South & Southern African Literature

A Review

Editor:	Eldred Durosimi Jones
Assistant Editor:	Marjorie Jones
Associate Editors:	Simon Gikandi
	Nnadozie Inyama
	Francis Imbuga
	Emmanuel Ngara
	Ato Quayson
Reviews Editor:	James Gibbs

JAMES CURREY
OXFORD

AFRICA WORLD PRESS
TRENTON, N.J.

James Currey Ltd
73 Botley Rd
Oxford OX2 0BS

Africa World Press, Inc.
PO Box 1892
Trenton NJ 08607

1 2 3 4 5 06 05 04 03 02

British Library Cataloguing in Publication Data
South & Southern African literature : a review. - (African
  literature today ; 23)
  1. South African literature - 20th century - History and
  criticism
  I. Jones, Eldred Durosimi, 1925- II. Jones, Marjorie
  809.8'968

ISBN 0-85255-523-7 (James Currey paper)

Typeset in 9/10 pt Melior by Long House Publishing Services, Cumbria, UK
Printed in the United States of America

Contents

vi   *Contents*

AFTERWORD

REVIEWS

Editorial Article
South & Southern African Literature

Eldred D. Jones

The dismantling of legal apartheid has liberated the culture and with it
the languages and literatures of South Africa into the outside world. It has
also freed the country itself from a monumental block which limited the
creative imagination by forcing it into a posture of reaction against an all-
pervasive oppressive system. The dominating influence in South African
literature, indeed, in all South African culture, has been apartheid. Its
stark polarities of black versus white, oppression versus liberty and
poverty versus opulence, have produced a literature of protest which is
limiting even in its compelling necessity. As Njabulo Ndebele argues in
Rediscovery of the Ordinary, it is a culture whose main feature is an exte-
riority which is reflected in the literature. The mere cataloguing of the
obvious surfaces of things and the self-evident inequities have hitherto
constituted a protest. But the coincidence of protest politics and protest
literature has been overtaken by events. Now shorn of its inhibitions, the
literature must assume a wider and deeper responsibility.

Continuing the argument, Ndebele suggests that an injection of irony,
hitherto largely absent from the output of South African writers, would
contribute to the production of an artistic tradition. What is required is a
new vision, the transcendence of the protest posture 'to extend the range
of personal and social experience as far as possible in order to contribute
to bringing about a highly conscious, sensitive new person in a new
society'. South African literature should rediscover the 'ordinary' which
includes a concern with the rural environment, and liberate itself from
the mesmerising lure of the township: 'the Jim come to Johannesburg'
syndrome.

That the 'ordinary' has not been entirely missing from South African
literature does not diminish the main force of Ndebele's argument – the
phrase 'largely missing' suggests his own awareness of this. The lure of
the townships is certainly a dominating one. In this regard, the work of
Sindiwe Magona is significant in its occasional handling of the 'ordinary'
in the rural context. But even the autobiography of this remarkable black
South African woman whose life – from premature motherhood and an

almost statusless existence under the double jeopardy of the apartheid system and African traditional society – is dominated by the Bantu Education Act and the segregation laws under which life was disrupted with whole communities being dislocated and relocated. She does succeed, however, in seeing herself as part of international womanhood:

> Although I did not know it then, by the time I reached home I had joined the invisible league of women, worldwide – the bearers and nurturers of the human race whom no government or institution recognizes or rewards, and no statistician captures and classifies. (175)

Sindiwe Magona's voice was part of the voice of black protest, a voice which found its echoes in the works of writers from other races. Lionel Abrahams, for example, was tortured with white guilt, but frustrated by an inability to go down the full road of liberation. Such tortured consciences as his would also enjoy the fruits of liberation. The end of the war of liberation and the consequent independence of Zimbabwe have not resulted in tranquillity of either consciousness or conscience. Uncomfortable questions of inequality – privileged versus underprivileged, men versus women, black on black oppression – form the basis of the work of writers like Chenjerai Hove and Yvonne Vera. The latter portrays women who bear the heavy burden of secrecy in a traditional society which refuses to acknowledge the heinousness of the crime of rape. Three generations of women suffer in uncomfortable silence, oppressed and frustrated. How does one express the inexpressible? How does one portray the horrors of incestuous rape without prurience or the inhuman violence and the futility of war without resort to journalistic sensationalism? Yvonne Vera has chosen the technique of metaphor rather than that of sequential realistic narration. The tongue is the vehicle of speech, the repository of memory; the tongue is a river but a river whose free flow is impeded by the traditional imposition of secrecy.

> Can a woman not speak the word that oppresses her heart, grows heavy on her tongue, heavy, pulling her to the ground? I do not speak and my word has grown roots on my tongue filling my mouth. Will my word grow into a tree while I water it everyday with silence? (44)

It is in this use of metaphor that the work of Yvonne Vera is distinguished from the documentary realism of Sindiwe Magona. Ndebele suggests the need for an injection of irony into the South African material; a greater injection of distancing metaphor might be another useful ingredient.

WORKS CITED

Magona, Sindiwe, *To My Children's Children*, Cape Town: David Philip, 1990.
Ndebele, Njabulo, *Rediscovery of the Ordinary*, Johannesburg: COSAW, 1991.
Vera, Yvonne, *Under the Tongue*, Harare: Baobab Books, 1996.

'Renaissance' & South African Writing

Lekan Oyegoke

In the rather uneasy relationship between creative writing and literary criticism in Africa in recent years, history has come to play a major role in the shaping of cultural directions. This might at first sound paradoxical – which influences the other, history or culture? – but a closer look reveals the fact that history is not only a record of events but also the events themselves. Hitherto, both the creative writing and the criticism of it have tended to treat history as some dumb subject, some immobile object of rust, dust and cobwebs. In subtle ways like this the manipulation of history is achieved. It must be pointed out, however, that in Africa the prostitution of history did not start with political independence but with the precolonial invasion of Africa by Europeans.

A rehash of the unsavoury details of how European invaders desecrated the history and cultures of Africa is neither necessary nor expedient in this short essay. The unhappy phenomenon is already well-documented by scholars such as Cheikh Anta Diop, Walter Rodney, Basil Davidson and a host of other historians, Africanists and literary theorists. The facts are well known and acknowledged. It has become a bit hackneyed to state that history was manipulated in order to provide moral and intellectual justification for the enslavement of Africans, then the trans-Atlantic slave trade, and latterly European colonialism and neo-colonialism in Africa. It is, moreover, now a generally accepted fact that these rapacious activities of assault and invasion once begun could not have been sustained if African history had not first been bulldozed, dismantled and then reassembled into a suitable new shape that was as far away from the truth as the sun is from the earth.

Nevertheless, it is equally true to assert that, even at those terrible times, history has had its brighter moments, and a good part is closely associated with literature. History has walked the hard road to redemption, to freedom, in literature, from such half-hearted attempts in the likes of Joseph Conrad's *Heart of Darkness* (1902) to more full-throttled efforts as in Chinua Achebe's *Things Fall Apart* (1958) and the acclaimed literary works by such authors as Ayi Kwei Armah, Camara

1

Laye, Es'kia Mphahlele, Peter Abrahams, Mazisi Kunene, Dennis Brutus.

There is, however, a surprising piece of paradox in the attitude to history of a part of pre-independence literary theory and criticism, the attitude captured in particular in the term, Negritude, and another, pan-Africanism. As many a critic has remarked, history was for the Negritude philosophy of African cultural experience a static sighting-post for idealism and romanticism. Similarly, pan-Africanism, taking its cue from Negritude, has ended up with an unreal, unrealistic and Utopian view of the African political and cultural experience by in its own case adopting a monolithic African cultural landscape. Different shades and characters of Afrocentricism have since emerged, more vocal, more strident than both Negritude and pan-Africanism, and attempted to perpetuate the fallacy of a static and unchanging African literary universe, the myth of a fixed, immobile and undynamic history.

This essay attempts an examination of the place of history in African culture, with South Africa as a specific example, by looking at change as an inevitable part of history and hence culture. The essay examines some of the potential consequences of change in the dynamics of South African literary culture and aesthetics. The word 'renaissance' has recently surfaced in the South African political vocabulary. Is it perhaps another word for 'change'?

I When in the mid-1960s Professor Lewis Nkosi denounced the tendency to propaganda in South African writing there was an outcry on the part of the scholars of African literature, not the least from the Marxist theorists and critics of African literature. The debate which Nkosi's observation generated led to a re-examination of certain concepts: propaganda as opposed to literature; the protest element as opposed to the aesthetic quality; commitment in literature. What did it mean? Should commitment mean one thing for a writer from the political vantage point of post-independence West or East Africa and another thing for a writer operating under the rank burden of suppression, repression and exploitation in apartheid South Africa? These were some of the questions raised and needless to say unresolved.

It is in the nature of literature to harbour ambiguity, controversy and inconclusiveness, such that time and again an old problem might with profit be revisited. In much the same way that Mphahlele's *Down Second Avenue* (1959) or Alan Paton's *Cry the Beloved Country* (1948) may be returned to for a second or the umpteenth round of interest, entertainment, reflection and information. The film industry backed by decades of experience in the ways of popular taste in cultural matters has already embarked on refilmings of Paton's famous novel.

Two items still hold out an interest to me in the issue raised by Nkosi. First, how valid is it to assert that South African literature in the early years of apartheid amounted to little more than propaganda? To answer this question we must look to history. The sociology of literature requires that we pay attention to the relations between the individual authors and the distinctive circumstances of the political and cultural conditions under which they wrote. The political sociology of apartheid was such that all that it invited from those on the wrong side of it was protest by any means available – the pen, fists and legs. The unique circumstances of apartheid would appear therefore to tend to blunt the strict division between literature and propaganda, in such a way that the two kinds of writing become only two sides of the same coin.

Second – and the product of history is the question closely related to the earlier one on the issue of commitment varying in terms of space or spatial conditioning – does commitment also vary in time, principally between the apartheid and post-apartheid eras? In short, is there any reason why the author writing under apartheid conditions should write differently after the collapse of apartheid?

Again here history remains the final arbiter as a lot will depend on the difference between the professed collapse of the apartheid system and the ontological reality of the dismantling of its structures. In short, the commitment of the writer in the new South Africa will depend on how much of the negative old order has been allowed to survive into the new South Africa. For example, Alex La Guma in *The Stone Country* (1967) portrays life in South Africa for the majority of its peoples as life in a vast concrete prison yard: cold, forbidding and heartless. In the stone country everything is hard, harsh and abrasive. The ruling class is rough, arrogant and self-centred. The law governing human social intercourse is akin to the law of the jungle given a veneer of morality, decency and civilisation. There is a predator/prey principle in the human relationships and the stone walls which effectively separate apartheid South Africa from the rest of the world assist in the promotion and perpetuation of medieval values of behaviour in the stone country.

The minority ruling class in the novel is aptly represented as a callous, snobbish, overconfident cat that sadistically toys with the mouse in the captivity of its bloodied claws. The mouse appears defenceless, puny and seemingly weak in contrast to the towering, intimidating might of the cat. In a fit of hubris the cat gets careless and the sharp-witted mouse leaps out into freedom. Deprived of its prey the cat is left in a fit of pique. This symbolic representation of the reality of life under apartheid between the oppressor and the oppressed has in retrospect proved prognostic. La Guma's fictional representation of so close a reality has been prophetic. Nevertheless, what the prophecy does not clarify and what history is only beginning to reveal is the kind of freedom into which the mouse escapes. The question then is, were La Guma to rewrite this novel after 1994 would he feel inclined to change anything? Has the stone country been pulled down and rebuilt with the milk of human kindness? Is the cat still

strutting about in the over-confident, arrogant knowledge of its might? Is
the mouse that escaped into freedom from the jaws of imminent death,
from the paws of the cat, able to go about the legitimate business of living
without skulking and looking over its shoulder? In short, has history
changed anything?

If the old order is still very much a part of the new in South Africa and
sheer arrogance struts about the streets in the wrong-headed belief that
the world was made for only one colour and that hate and not love is
God's greatest commandment to man or that the principle governing
human conduct should be 'live and let die', then in post-1994 South
Africa as in the proper apartheid years the anguish and suffering occa-
sioned by the physical and social decimation of families in *Cry the
Beloved Country* (1948) will retain a contemporary rather than a historical
value. The inhumanity and callousness recorded by Can Themba in *The
Will to Die* (1972) will remain contemporaneous and not historical in a
formal sense; the humiliation, dehumanisation and resistance explored in
Nadine Gordimer's *Burger's Daughter* (1979) will retain a contemporary
rather than historical connection with reality.

Nevertheless, commitment in literature may not always be viewed
from the political or sociological angle. Commitment in arts is also
amenable to more flexible usages. A writer may choose to define a sense
of commitment as an individual attitude to the arts or literature, as the
body of aesthetic requirements the fulfilment of which is necessary for
the production of 'good' art or 'good' literature. This kind of writer will
insist on the imaginative content in literature as the yardstick for its eval-
uation. The writer for whom aesthetic concerns are paramount will make
all other considerations in the production of literature subservient to the
eternal laws of literature having to do with beauty, balance and the
sublime. A literary critic who is similarly disposed will also be inclined
to separate good from bad literature, literature from propaganda and
history, imaginative writing from the oral traditions. In this connection,
the separation may be undertaken for all literary works written during the
apartheid era and for those after that period, separating them on either
side of 1994, the momentous watermark of South African political
history.

II In talking about South African literature there has been the tendency
to shift perspectives. Prior to 1994 South African writing had been
treated by the rest of free Africa mostly as black South African writing,
which had the effect of either excluding liberal white writers who were
sympathetic to the black cause or accommodating them in an uneasy kind
of relationship. Writing in Afrikaans was as a rule ignored in black
African literary studies, and as a result the writings of some liberal
Afrikaner writers were excluded from the mainstream of literary interest

and scholarly concern in the rest of Africa. Inevitably, works by the likes of André Brink were generally ignored, even by those scholars who were sceptical about a narrow political or sociological view of commitment in literature.

As it turned out, literary scholarship in the rest of Africa endorsed by tacit agreement a view of South African literature which tied it up with the issue of relevance. First, South African writing must be socially relevant given its context of apartheid politics, and second, the acceptable and accepted notion of relevance must pertain to the dismantling of the apartheid system and its replacement with a just, democratic, and humane system. The appeal of this position, in which South African literature was defined in terms of its 'social relevance', explains the inclusion of such non-black South African writers as Athol Fugard and Nadine Gordimer, not to mention Alan Paton, in the South African literary canon, even in the height of apartheid under John Vorster and P.W. Botha.

From the point of view of protest or social relevance, Fugard's plays score very high marks, and as socially and politically relevant texts his works have been eminently successful going by, if nothing else, the frequency of banning orders, arrests, prohibitions and other forms of state harassment of this citizen. *Sizwe Bansi is Dead* (1972), for instance, captures the dire circumstances under which blacks lived in the heyday of apartheid. The play is arresting not so much because of the action (there isn't much of this) but because of the sordid details and truths it reveals about apartheid.

Paton's *Too Late, the Phalarope* (1953) is a moving tale about the devastating consequences of irrational laws on individual life, family unity, and social and racial harmony. The novel is a powerful dramatisation of how the Immorality Act under the apartheid system served to destroy lives and ruin promising careers in South Africa. But because the protagonist in this novel is not only a white policeman but also an Afrikaner the novel has not enjoyed as much attention as *Cry the Beloved Country* (1948) in the rest of Africa. Yet, from the point of view of the aesthetic, involving balance, suspense, surprise, plot, the evocation of atmosphere and feeling, and the general cohesion of its parts it would appear to me to be as interesting as *Cry the Beloved Country*.

This point again appears to underscore the importance of relevance in South African literature. Writing has to be pro-majority, as it were, for it to qualify as South African literature. This attitude is natural, if not altogether logical, and may be reduced to a formula: there is an inhuman situation in force involving sectional interests whereby the minority takes it upon itself to speak for the rest; therefore ignore this smaller interest for the purpose of discussing South African literature – acknowledge it only where it is concerned with the issues of justice, fair play and liberty.

Since 1994 it has become much easier to define South African literature and, as in the spheres of economics and politics, South Africa has transformed itself into a touchstone of culture that the rest of Africa may learn something from. With impressive speed South Africa has moved from unsuccessful attempts in 1976 to impose Afrikaans on all, to a more decent position involving the recognition and official elevation of the major indigenous African languages spoken or used in South Africa. South African literature has now potentially become the totality of the literatures written in South Africa in all the languages of South Africa.

By contrast the rest of (black) Africa has continued illusorily to define African writing strictly in terms of the inherited languages of colonialism, namely, English, French and Portuguese mainly, whilst in most cases officially ignoring the indigenous African languages and their literatures. Attempts to define African literature have accordingly foundered on a quicksand of cultural fallacies and contradictions. The political transition from colonialism to self-rule in Africa has not always been accompanied by a corresponding cultural transformation, with the result that at the political and economic levels stability was not always possible.

Given South Africa's recent positive scores in these areas and (black) Africa's regrettable disregard of the problem, social (and cultural) relevance in writing is not without its uses. Still, social and cultural relevance is subject to the march of time, is subject to change.

III The element of change has not in my opinion been accorded the respect which it deserves by some of the critical theorists of African literature. For instance, the 1980s successor to Negritude, Afrocentricism, argues stridently for a return to the African past for literary models without allowance being made for the ontological difference between the modern African writer and the oral traditional bard. It argues also that the written imaginative forms be judged almost entirely by criteria deriving from folklore.

This confusion is the result, as has been mentioned, of the adoption of a static, myopic view of history and culture. The modern writer is seen as the (logical) clone of the traditional bard now in the process of fossilisation in near historical time. The piece of fossil, from the viewpoint of this philosophy, is on the verge of extinction. The part about extinction is correct, it must be admitted, but as a result not of fossilisation, but of modernity and the advent of literacy. As the various cultures of Africa acquire increasing literacy the relative significance of the oral bard proportionately falls. This is a natural process, the consequence of change.

Nevertheless, it happens also to be true that for most parts of (black) Africa a large percentage of the population is still locked in a culture of orality. Oral literature scholars such as Walter J. Ong and Ruth Finnegan point out, however, that for many cultures in Africa there is a mutual co-existence of orality and literacy. This is actually an observable fact in Africa. Hence, the reality is a situation involving the modern writer and the oral bard or performer fulfilling two separate roles in culture and society, each role no less legitimate than the other; and given which premise, the oral bard is entitled to as big a claim on recognition as the writer in the modern context and is no more historical than the writer except in the sense of having been around for much longer in Africa. Thus the oral traditions are not a part of culture left behind and lost in time but are also a part of the present experience in Africa.

In South Africa there have been a few attempts to capture the magic of orality in print, as in Kunene's *Emperor Shaka The Great* (1977), but a lot has yet to be done, and post-haste, because of the inefficiency of orality at self-preservation and self-perpetuation. Nowadays, the oral performance cannot only be captured and preserved in print, the performance together with the oral moment of delivery – lost to print – can also be captured and preserved on film with very little lost in the process.

There appears to be the general assumption that the collapse of apartheid in South Africa will lead automatically to increased literary output. That more creative writing will result from the experience of freedom and the enfranchisement of the majority. This assumption may be examined from different perspectives. First, there is the observation that the creative impulse is sometimes born out of unsavoury circumstances of deprivation and suffering as was commonplace under the apartheid system. This, however, assumes a prior acquisition of literacy, the importance of which the apartheid regime recognised and made sure it did everything possible to prevent the black majority from having. Were this not the case, according to this view, South Africa would by now have been flooded with imaginative black literature inspired and informed by the inhuman circumstances of life under apartheid. This theory probably explains why, in Nigeria today, for example, there is an unprecedented upsurge of cultural creativity now that the national economy has been ruined by years of mismanagement, incompetence and ineptitude on the part of the government since political independence, leaving in its wake poverty, disenchantment and disillusionment.

Second, the obverse of the first, there is the view that the satisfaction or euphoria of achieved goals, be they individual or collective, begets a sense of contentment that works at crosspurposes to the creative impulse. Material comfort tends to nurture indolence generally and is thus a disincentive to creativity. By this disputable argument increased material and psychological comfort in South Africa after 1994 could undermine the desire and discipline required for writing. And given that the bulk of writing prior to 1994 had been of the 'protest' kind and the circumstances that engendered it are no longer there, there might seem to be little reason left for the majority of South Africans to want to write after 1994.

There is, however, the caveat that now there will be greater enlightenment as the country relentlessly pursues the goal of compulsory education for the previously educationally disadvantaged masses. And judging from the experience with creativity in the enlightened, more affluent, and more comfortable societies of the world, there is no reason why creativity should not be compatible with easy material, social and psychological circumstances. Hence, the golden age of South African literature seems to be on this side of 1994, yet to arrive.

IV The golden age of South African literature is on the way as the whole country undergoes mental, psychological and spiritual rebirth. This renaissance will not come about as dramatically as the first multiracial general elections; it will be slower but steadier as old self-destructive prejudices and passions melt away and get replaced with more humane and civilised attitudes which recognise and respect the right of all human beings to life, dignity and decent treatment. For years the white South African had been seen by black South Africans as some kind of monster equipped with an unlimited capacity for irrational hatred of others not of his colour. This unlimited capacity for unnatural hate has been described as actually a form of incapacity. Kwame Anthony Appiah (1992) describes it as 'cognitive incapacity':

> This cognitive incapacity is not, of course, a rare one. Many of us are unable to give up beliefs that play a part in justifying the special advantages we gain from our positions in the social order. Many people who express extrinsic racist beliefs – many white South Africans, for example – are beneficiaries of social orders that deliver advantages to them in virtue of their 'race', so that their justification for those advantages is just an instance of this general phenomenon. (p. 14)

This point is vividly illustrated in M.R. Ridley's critical review of certain 'informed' reactions or attitudes to Shakespeare's great tragedy, *Othello*, some of which had concluded that Shakespeare was too correct a delineator of human nature to have coloured Othello black (p. li). In the face of overwhelming evidence to the contrary some white critics of Shakespeare hold that Othello, the black eponymous hero of one of the greatest plays of the Renaissance period, is white or not-black.

The one seen as a 'monster' decides the other is a savage or is simply subhuman. When 'monsters' and 'savages' find themselves living together the result is a riot of fists, stabbings, gunshots and mayhem. But when, confronted with the mind-boggling variety of the Creator's works, men acknowledge this as evidence that God couldn't have intended the earth for only one colour, the result is humility, love, peace and progress. Ridley's observation here is equally apt:

> now a good deal of the trouble arises, I think, from a confusion of colour and contour. To a great many people the word 'negro' suggests at once the picture of what they would call a 'nigger', the wooly hair, thick lips, round skull, blunt features, and burntcork blackness of the traditional nigger minstrel. Their subconscious generalization is as silly as that implied in Miss Preston's 'the African

race' or Coleridge's 'veritable negro'. There are more races than one in Africa, and that a man is black in colour is no reason why he should, even to European eyes, look sub-human. One of the finest heads I have ever seen on any human being was that of a negro conductor on an American Pullman car. He had lips slightly thicker than an ordinary European's, and he had somewhat curly hair; for the rest he had a long head, a magnificent forehead, a keenly chiselled nose, rather sunken cheeks, and his expression was grave, dignified, and a trifle melancholy. He was coal-black, but he might have sat to a sculptor for a statue of Caesar, or, so far as appearance went, have played a superb Othello. (p. li)

By the admission of some South Africans of all shades there is as yet a wall of ignorance separating black, white and other South Africans, the collapse of apartheid structures notwithstanding. The removal of this ignorance will in my opinion be the driving force and mainstay of new South African literature together with a general celebration of life. As the writers seize the day and advance into the golden age of South African literature, the readership must be kept in tow. African literature must be included in the educational curriculum at every level. In other words, South Africans, black and white, should be familiar with not only Shakespeare, Dickens and Milton, but also Mphahlele, Kunene, Brutus, Mbulelo Mzamane, Miriam Tlali, Christine Qunta, and so on and so forth.

The writers, readers, critics, and publishers must rise above the mush of conceptual fallacies and ignorance upon which African literature has been founded and realise, as Achebe has pointed out, that African literature is not 'African literature' alone but a literature in three important parts: (i) African literature written in English, French, Portuguese; (ii) indigenous writing in the several languages of Africa, for example, Akan, Gikuyu, Sotho, Tsonga, Yoruba, Xhosa, Zulu – languages as important as the languages of Europe; and (iii) oral performance. The audiences differ for these three categories of literature. It is only against this background that there can be a truly meaningful renaissance of African literature.

It should seem obvious that by having a large sophisticated economy South Africa may be said to be ready for its golden age of literature, having as it does an advanced publishing infrastructure. But there are other factors. However, its self-inflicted weakness, that of a large uneducated populace, is being speedily corrected through sheer will-power and collective determination.

On a different level, there is an admirable corporate response to the needs of the arts by the world of private business: Until recently Gilbeys sponsored a Bertrams VO Literature of Africa Award which led to a harvest of new literary works or, at least, new unpublished manuscripts submitted by newer as well as experienced writers, with the sponsors working in concert with publishing partners in the now (surprisingly) defunct Skotaville Publishers. There are also the Sanlam-sponsored book and publishing prizes to recognise new South African writing and new South African publishing, such as Vivlia Publishers and Booksellers who won it for their publication *She Plays with the Darkness* (1995) by Zakes

Mda. The South African *Sunday Times*-sponsored Alan Paton Book Award aims to stimulate writing in the non-fiction genre of literature (autobiography, biography, etc, – a past winner being Nelson Mandela's *Long Walk to Freedom* 1994).

Apart from prizes and awards sponsored by some of the publishing houses themselves to stimulate writing, private business has continued to support the arts in general and literature in particular in some other ways that may be unaccompanied by the flourish of trumpets or cheap publicity in favour of the sponsor. A new creative writing journal named *TurfWRITE* has been launched by The University of the North's office of the Dramatist-in-Residence – 'a post kindly funded by Anglo American and De Beers chairman's fund' (*TurfWRITE*, inside back cover). According to the journal's editor, it is 'to guarantee space for authors from this province which has long suffered from publishing marginalisation and creative writing inexposure' ('Editorial Note', p.5). Sponsors like these are sensitive to the needs of the arts and genuinely committed to their promotion in South Africa.

Still, as some writers have observed, creative writing must remain a labour of love that should not depend on the possibility of a literary prize or an award for its production. The award or prize if and when it comes must be for the writer incidental to the process of writing, and not be the reason for writing. Far more important than the book prize or award is a good reading culture that guarantees that a literary work worthy of the description will be read. There is reason to believe that there is a reading culture in South Africa, despite the onslaught on it by a contrary television culture, only its spread is not commensurate with the size and distribution of its population. Hence, for it to be meaningful a cultural reawakening in South Africa must begin with a concerted and purposeful cultivation of the book market. This, as has been noted, is beginning to happen and it is in this context that talk of an African or a South African renaissance makes sense.

WORKS CITED

Appiah, Kwame Anthony, *In My Father's House: Africa in the Philosophy of Culture*, New York, Oxford: Oxford University Press, 1992.
Diop, Cheikh Anta, *The African Origin of Civilisation: Myth or Reality*, New York and Westport, Conn.: Lawrence Hill and Company, 1974.
Nkosi, Lewis, *Tasks and Masks*, London: Longman, 1981.
—— *The Transplanted Heart*, Benin City: Ethiope, 1975.
Ong, Walter J., *Orality and Literacy: The 'Technologizing' of the Word*, London: Methuen, 1982.
Ridley, M.R. (ed.), *Othello*, The Arden Shakespeare, London: Methuen, 1958.
Ruganda, John (ed.), *TurfWRITE: A Creative Writing Journal* 1: 1 September 1998.

The Changing Role of Poetry in the Struggle for Freedom, Justice & Equality in South Africa

Ritske Zuidema

The history of black political protest and resistance against apartheid in South Africa is a long and turbulent one. Nevertheless, it can be argued that, until the late 1960s, protest actions hardly ever posed a serious challenge to the military power of the authorities. This changed in 1968 with the emergence of the Black Consciousness Movement and its radical ideology of black pride and self-assertion. Black Consciousness played a major role in sowing the seeds of the ferocious and highly successful resistance campaigns that rocked the country in the 1970s and 1980s. These resistance campaigns eventually forced the authorities to give in, abandon the widely despised system of apartheid, and start negotiations with the opposition movement that led the country to majority rule in 1994.

What is so interesting about South Africa's anti-apartheid struggle from a literary point of view is that, throughout these years of heightened political resistance, literature played an important role. Poetry in particular was widely used as a means of conscientising the masses and rallying them behind the political programmes of the organisations that led the anti-apartheid struggle. Interestingly enough, poetry continued to be closely linked to the wider social and political processes of the country even after the changes of the 1990s. It is my aim in this article to describe very precisely how after 1968 poetry came to be used as a 'consciousness raiser' and 'a weapon in the struggle', what kind of formal demands this 'commitment' placed on the poet, how the different ideological phases of South Africa's liberation struggle affected the contents of black South African poetry, and what influence the political transformations of the 1990s have had on its scope and direction.

Poetry started to play a significant role in South Africa's social and political struggles at the time when Steve Biko's Black Consciousness Movement came to dominate black opposition politics in South Africa, in the late 1960s and early 1970s. According to Steve Biko, the main aim of Black Consciousness was:

> to make the black man come to himself; to pump back life into his empty shell;
> to infuse him with pride and dignity, to remind him of his complicity in the
> crime of allowing himself to be misused and therefore letting evil reign supreme
> in the country of his birth.[1]

In Biko's opinion, the black man in South Africa needed to be psychologically liberated from his apartheid-induced inferiority complex before he could liberate himself politically. For this campaign of psychological liberation to proceed successfully, the message of Black Consciousness had to be spread to all layers of South Africa's black community. Hence, Black Consciousness activists were in need of a medium through which they could spread their political message in a quick and effective manner. They chose culture in general and poetry in particular. Various kinds of cultural gatherings were organised at which the masses were conscientised by means of political speeches, drama and poetry. As the South African scholar Kelwyn Sole argues:

> Literature and drama were used as a means of political and cultural communication and conscientization, an attempt at 'dynamic communal discussion' by artists determined to inform all sections of black society of their position as blacks in South Africa, to give them encouragement and to awaken, unify and mobilize them under the rubric of black identity.[2]

The choice of poetry as the most favoured medium of political conscientisation was not surprising. Poems could be performed orally in front of large audiences, and because of their brevity and density they could be turned into effective carriers of urgent political messages. Moreover, oral poetry had traditionally played a highly significant role in the cultures of the various communities that made up South Africa's black population.

A notable example of such a Black Consciousness-inspired poem was Don Mattera's 'No time, black man' which was written in 1972:

Stand Black man,
Put that cap back
On your beaten head

Look him in the eye
Cold and blue
Like the devil's fire
Tell him enough,
Three centuries is more
Than you take,
          Enough...
Let him hear it
If he turns his face and sneers
Spit and tell him shit
It's all or nothing;
He's got all
And you have nothing

Don't bargain with oppression
There's no time man,

Just no more time
For the Black man
To fool around... [3]

What is striking about Mattera's poem is that it addresses an audience of ordinary black South Africans rather than the intellectual fringe of society that most conventional European poets tend to write for. With this audience in mind, Mattera has done his best to present his message in the most simple and straightforward way possible. Linguistically, the poem is not complex. Mattera uses plain English in order to make sure that those with only limited knowledge of the English language can understand him. Unlike many of the poets who were active in the previous decades, he has no inclination to sound particularly formal, opaque or 'poetic' or to show off about his exquisite knowledge of the English language. His commitment is obviously not to academics, intellectuals and literary critics, but to 'the masses'.

It is, however, not only the language of Mattera's poem that displays a high degree of simplicity and straightforwardness. He has also attempted to simplify the rather sophisticated argumentation of the Black Consciousness Movement by capturing the complex political reality of South Africa in a clear-cut them–us opposition. The black and white communities in South Africa are homogenised and presented as two individuals who are addressed as 'he' (the white man) and 'you' (the black man). Mattera contrasts the social positions of the two communities in a simple, but highly effective way, claiming that 'He's got all/And you have nothing'. In other words, there is an imbalance that needs to be addressed, and it is the black man who has to do it. He has to muster the courage and strength to stand up, shout his defiance right into the white man's face and take what is rightfully his.

Thus, by using plain and simple language to convey a complex political message, Mattera has managed to create 'a people's poem', a poem that is addressed to the community as a whole and does not exclude the ordinary man in the street. In South Africa, 'people's poetry' was in many ways synonymous with 'oral poetry'. The masses in South Africa were not regular buyers or readers of volumes of written poetry. Their culture was still predominantly oral. If, therefore, a poet wished to address and communicate with 'the people' he or she needed to make a very conscious choice for a poetry that could be used effectively for oral declamation.

In Mattera's poem, this emphasis on the oral communication of poetry is clearly noticeable. Although the poem exists in written form, it is not particularly suitable for private reading. The language it uses is the language of the spoken address, not the language of private contemplation. The poet presents himself as a public orator who speaks directly to his audience in an attempt to incite them to action. Note the dominance of imperative grammatical structures in the poem in sentences like 'Stand black man/Put that cap back on your beaten head/Look him in the eye/ Tell him enough'. This dominance of imperative sentences reflects the poet's main aim of persuading his audience to take action.

Another poet who used his poetry for similar purposes was James Matthews. In 1971, he published his collection *Cry Rage* which contained the remarkable poem 'Freedom's child':

> Freedom's child
> you have been denied too long
> fill your lungs and cry rage
> step forward and take your rightful place
> you're not going to grow up
> knocking at the back door
> for you there will be no travelling
> third class enforced by law
> with segregated schooling and sitting on the floor
> the rivers of our land, mountain tops
> and the shore
> it is yours, you will not be denied anymore
> Cry rage, freedom's child.[4]

Like Mattera, Matthews speaks directly to his fellow blacks in a simple, clear and straightforward way. 'Freedom's Child' is meant to bring about a change of attitude in South Africa's black community. He urges blacks to leave the years of apathy and inactivity behind and to force themselves back on South Africa's political stage. Hence, the powerful lines 'you have been denied too long/fill your lungs and cry rage/step forward and take your rightful place' which are comparable to Mattera's calls on his fellow blacks to 'stand' and 'put that cap back/on your beaten head'. In both cases, poetry is used as a powerful means of breaking the enforced silence of the 1960s, awaking the black man from his slumber, pumping 'back life into his empty shell'[5] and preparing him for the battles to come.

The emergence of the philosophy of Black Consciousness was extremely important in the history of black resistance in South Africa. After the dark years of fear and repression that followed the Sharpeville massacre of 1961, it was Black Consciousness that instilled new pride and determination in a battered population. It provided South Africa's black community with the confidence that was needed to wage new resistance campaigns against their oppression. In fact, many scholars have argued very persuasively that it was Black Consciousness that sowed the seeds of the Soweto uprising that rocked the country in 1976 and the more formidable uprisings of the 1980s.

During these uprisings, as in the Black Consciousness years, poetry played an important role as a 'consciousness raiser' and inciter of the masses. Again, black poets saw it as their primary task to guide the struggle in the appropriate direction and enhance the spirit of resistance and militant defiance in their community. Interestingly enough, however, the ideological position of most of these poets was no longer directly related to the views of the Black Consciousness Movement. In the early 1970s, Black Consciousness achieved its aim of psychologically re-awakening and liberating black South Africa. A new spirit of black pride and self-reliance had firmly taken root. The time had therefore come to move away from the psychological battles, and fight the real, physical battles for the political liberation of black South Africa. In this new phase of the struggle, other organisations came to dominate South Africa's opposition movement. The most important of these were the ANC, its armed wing, Umkhonto we Sizwe, and the United Democratic Front, a broad coalition of anti-apartheid organisations which were united in their support for the political principles of the ANC as stated in the Freedom Charter. Ideologically, the main differences between the ANC and the Black Consciousness Movement were that the ANC tended to be more socialist-oriented and more willing to work together with progressive elements in South Africa's white community than the Black Consciousness Movement. Moreover, due to its long history of protest and resistance against white minority rule, the ANC was much better equipped to provide leadership to an intensified campaign of resistance and defiance.

Perhaps even more than the Black Consciousness leaders, the ANC leaders were aware of the possibility of turning culture into a 'weapon of the struggle'. In 1982, for example, the ANC was the main organiser behind a large cultural conference called 'Culture and Resistance' which was held in Gaborone, Botswana. At this conference, over 800 South African cultural workers pledged their allegiance to the liberation struggle and vowed to dedicate their cultural work entirely to furthering the struggle of the ANC and Umkhonto we Sizwe.

Thus, the way was paved for a type of poetry that was almost purely propagandistic in nature. It was a poetry that was written entirely at the service of the armed struggle and that sought to give firm support to the ideology of the ANC. Many of the poets who emerged during these volatile years of intensified political resistance and guerrilla warfare were not poets *pur sang*. They saw poetry as part of a wider programme of political and cultural resistance, and tended to combine literary activities with political activism for the ANC, Umkhonto we Sizwe, the United Democratic Front or the trade union movement.

One of these new poets who emerged in the 1980s was Dikobe wa Mogale. Dikobe was a fighter in Umkhonto we Sizwe and used his poetry as a means of describing, commenting on and, most importantly, propagating the armed struggle he was involved in. The title poem of his first collection 'baptism of fire' illustrates very clearly how in the person of Dikobe wa Mogale armed resistance and poetic writing become intertwined and complement each other:

once more
we have been to isandlwana

to sharpen the spear
of the nation
in the winds teeth
at the altar
of heroic sacrifice
where the indomitable spirits
of warriors repose
and we have heard
the dead speak
with the echo of voices
leaping and raging
with tongues of fire
which flushed the sky
as rockets-bullets-and-blood
sang a lilting tune
steady like the rhythm
of blood rivers pulse
heaving with white skeletons
once more there is
venom in the mouth
of the oppressed
after the terror of bulhoek
the horror of sharpeville
the genocide of june 16th
and the endless massacre diplomacy
of kassinga, matola and maseru
once more
we have drunk our fill
from the bitter calabash of struggle
and made our offering
of liver and spleen
at the anvil of unity
we now chant
and sing your name
in a curse
you do not want to hear us
but our words
like a butchers knife
slash through your ears
the time has come
for you to reap
the whirlwind you sowed
for it is now
a harvest of fire
freedom
is once more
on the lips
of the oppressed
struggle breaks open
like an old wound
and bleeds afresh
the time has come
to strike and parry
deadly blows as we
make a final stand

digging heels
into the red flesh
of ancestral soil
overhead
iron sharpens iron
in a baptism of fire .[6]

'baptism of fire' is more than just a conventional protest or resistance poem. In fact, it could be defined more aptly as a form of war propaganda. With his poem Dikobe hopes to rally the physical and moral support of the black masses in South Africa behind the ANC's liberation war, and to encourage his fellow blacks to make the sacrifices that are needed to liberate the country. Like Mattera, therefore, Dikobe acts as a rhetorician who seeks to persuade an audience to adopt a particular point of view and to inspire them to follow a particular course of action.

With these aims in mind, Dikobe focuses on glorifying the struggle he is involved in and presenting it as the culmination of a long and heroic history of resistance against white minority rule in South Africa. The reference to the battle of Isandlwana in the poem's first line is significant in this respect. Isandlwana is the site where in 1879 a heroic battle was fought between a Zulu army led by king Cetshwayo and the British colonial forces. The Zulus defeated the British, and the battle became the pride of the history of black resistance in South Africa. In the poem, Dikobe subtly links this battle fought a hundred years ago with the battle fought by Umkhonto in the 1980s. As a result, the battle of the present becomes the rightful successor to that heroic battle of the past. It is implied that, just like that battle, it will end in a resounding victory for black South Africa.

In addition to Isandlwana, Dikobe refers to a number of other famous sites of the struggle in his poem. He mentions 'the terror of bulhoek/the horror of sharpeville/the genocide of june 16th/and the endless massacre diplomacy/of kassinga, matola and maseru'. By accumulating these powerful symbols of various phases of the struggle, Dikobe aims to instil a sense of historical consciousness in his audience and to remind them of the fact that the battles of the 1980s are not to be seen in isolation, but as part of a much longer history of heroic resistance. The battle being fought by him and his fellow Umkhonto fighters is presented as the last and most heroic episode of this long history that will finally bring the long-awaited dawn of liberation. The repetition of the key phrase 'once more' as a rhetorical device is significant in this respect. The implication is that only once more will the fighters take up their arms, and this time the victory will finally be theirs.

One of the poem's striking characteristics is its abundance of religious language. Dikobe refers to 'a baptism of fire', 'the altar of heroic sacrifice', and 'tongues of fire' and tells the oppressor to 'reap/the whirlwind you sowed'. This abundance of solemn and formal expressions with religious connotations serves to create the impression that the war fought by Dikobe and his Umkhonto comrades is much more than just a liberation struggle. It becomes a holy war, some sort of South African jihad. The implication is that it is everyone's duty to take part in this struggle and to be prepared to die for it, if necessary.

Not surprisingly, therefore, one of the poem's central images is the image of sacrifice. For Dikobe, the willingness to sacrifice oneself for the nation and its liberation struggle is the highest ideal that a black South African can achieve. It is at this 'altar of heroic sacrifice' that the freedom fighters of South Africa's anti-apartheid struggle can obtain a degree of immortality and can take the decisive steps that will eventually allow them to join the ranks of the heroic ancestors whose support is sought in the poem's first lines. In his article 'The Poetry of Dikobe wa Mogale', Colin Gardner provides further insights in the ways in which the Christian image of sacrifice is used by Dikobe to propagate the struggle:

> An important aspect of traditional Christian symbolism is that it always points forward: the most agonizing and dispiriting evocations of Christ's or of a Christ-like suffering turn out in the end, and against the odds, to be a prelude to resurrection, redemption, liberation. Suffering is important not in itself ... but as a way forward into a brighter future .[7]

This idea of redemption or liberation through sacrifice or prolonged suffering is central to the poem. In lines like 'once more/we have drunk our fill/from the bitter calabash of struggle' or 'struggle breaks open/like an old wound/and bleeds afresh', Dikobe shows that it is not his aim to make his audience believe that taking part in armed resistance is an altogether pleasant experience. What he argues is that in the circumstances under which the poem was written, waging armed resistance to white minority rule had become absolutely vital and indispensable for the continuation of a threatened society. The image of fire which is repeated several times in the poem is significant in this respect. In Dikobe's work, the fire is divorced from its conventional connotations, and is reinterpreted in a positive way. The fire of destruction is thus transformed into a cleansing force that purges society of evil and that will bring redemption and rebirth to South Africa's black community. The title, 'baptism of fire', has to be understood in this context. Undergoing the fire and destruction of armed struggle is like being baptised and is a prerequisite for rebirth and ultimate redemption.

Dikobe's poem has to be placed in a political context that was radically different from the one that spawned Mattera's 'No Time, Black Man'. In the latter, the black man still needed to be persuaded to look the white man in the eye and 'tell him shit'. In the volatile and highly charged atmosphere of the 1980s, however, this was no longer necessary. As Daniel P. Kunene argues in his article 'Language, Literature and the Struggle for Liberation in South Africa':

> When the struggle has progressed to a certain point, the demon of fear is conquered. The politics of fear are replaced by the politics of confrontation, for the oppressed can now speak to his oppressor from a position of equality.[8]

In the early 1970s, the liberation movement led by Black Consciousness activists was still mainly concerned with attempting to eradicate 'the politics of fear' and making the black man assertive enough to 'speak to his oppressor from a position of equality'. In the 1980s, this phase had already been passed. Dikobe's poem testifies to a new sense of triumph and confidence that had captured his community in the aftermath of the Soweto uprising of 1976, and that continued to push the struggle towards new heights of intensified resistance in the following decade. He shows great awareness of the strength he and his community possess and the formidable threat they can pose to the authorities. Thus the dominant feeling in Dikobe's poem is one of heroic anticipation of a coming victory: 'our words/like a butcher's knife/slash through your ears/the time has come/for you to reap/the whirlwind you sowed/for it is now/a harvest of fire'.

The kind of intensified resistance that South Africa's black community was prepared to wage against the oppressor in the 1980s was one of the factors that played a role in the decision of the apartheid government to make considerable concessions to the liberation movement, and start a process of negotiations in 1990. In the following four years, which are now known as the transition years, South Africa's black community was presented with new political challenges that were entirely different from the ones that dominated the previous decades. Because of the new commitments to a peaceful process of transition, the necessity for armed struggle against white minority rule had disappeared. Instead, an entirely different struggle had to be fought. During all the years of struggle and oppression, South Africa had become a society fraught with fissures, divisions, fear, distrust and traumatic memories of a brutal past. A new and truly free and democratic South Africa could therefore only arise if its people learnt to deal with their past, embraced a new spirit of reconciliation and unification, and were willing to build a new society based on the ideal of justice and prosperity for all.

In this long and difficult process, poetry once again came to play a significant role. As they had done in the previous decades, black poets took up the challenges that the new political circumstances presented them with. Once again, poetry came to serve a consciousness-raising purpose. This time, however, they were no longer speaking primarily to the black community, but to the South African nation as a whole. Their aim was no longer to convince black men of the need to take up arms and drive out the white settlers, but to persuade all the citizens of South Africa to embrace the much-needed spirit of reconciliation and adopt a commitment to building up a new, fair and inclusive South Africa. Thus, a shift took place in black South African poetry from a largely destructive approach that favoured the violent overthrow of an old despised political order to a more constructive one that focused on reconciliation, coopera- tion and community-building. One of the poems that has to be seen in the light of this new commitment to constructivism and reconciliation is Mongane Wally Serote's *Come and Hope With Me* which was published shortly before the elections of 1994. The poem is a passionate plea to the people of South Africa to stand together, stop their quarrelling and recog- nise the need to build a new world for themselves and their children.

> we do not want any civil war
> we do not want any racial or tribal war
> we do not want the spilling of blood
> we have known no peace
> we want the simple things of life
> to drink
> to eat
> to know
> to sing and to dance
> we want to return to dreams
> to desire
> to hope
> we want to work and to build
> we want to walk and to talk
> we must return to the will and wish to live[9]

The phrase that returns throughout the poem and its predecessor *Third World Express* is 'the simple things of life'. In essence, Serote is trying to make the people of South Africa aware of the very simple but at the same time very fundamental needs that they all share as humans. In Serote's view, it is the recognition of what all South Africans have in common that can form a solid foundation for a new, reconciled South Africa in which every individual and every ethnic group can take part and make its con- tribution for the betterment of society as a whole.

Such a commitment to the public rediscovery of common needs and aspirations in a highly polarised society lies at the heart of much of the poetry produced in the 1990s. One of the poets who clearly embodies this new form of social and political commitment is Seitlhamo Motsapi. Motsapi's strength lies in the highly subtle, but at the same time extremely effective way in which he manages to spread and advocate new moral and spiritual values that are linked to his society's need to reconcile and replace destructivism and polarisation with a new spirit of construc- tivism, cooperation and understanding. One of Motsapi's most famous poems is 'the man'.

It deals with a nameless man whose humbleness and humanity set the standards that, in Motsapi's view, the people of the new South Africa should aspire to.

> an almost forgotten acquaintance
> was in town recently

i noticed that it started raining
just as he ambled in

i remember him as a simple man
growing up, we all wanted
to be doctors, lawyers & teachers
so the blood could ebb out of the village

my friend had much more sober dreams
he asked the heavens to grant him
the imposing peace of the blue-gum in his backyard
& that all the poor send him their tears
so he could be humble like the sun
so the red wax of the stars would not drip on him

i remember that man today
& all i think of is his unassuming radiance
like that of a blushing angel
as for his dreams
he tells us
whole forests invade his sleep at night
so that there's only standing room
for the dreams[10]

There are few poets who manage to espouse a form of liberation from the divisions and quarrels of the past as effectively and genuinely as Motsapi does in his poem. To get his message across, Motsapi has chosen an allegorical approach. His simple and humble man epitomises the kind of spiritual and moral rebirth that he sees as the most potent cure for the problems that the emerging new South Africa is faced with. Significantly, Motsapi's man is not interested in playing political games or associating himself with any particular political movement or faction. Nor is he particularly eager to become part of a new assertive black bourgeoisie and pursue some high-flying career that will arouse the envy of his fellow men. On the contrary, he is content to remain 'human' and to develop his own humanity so as to be able to help his small community and the people around him. In that sense, his attitude to life is totally constructivist and cooperative in outlook. His 'unassuming radiance' therefore sets the standards which Motsapi sees as essential for the success of a new South Africa.

When comparing Motsapi's work to the poems of the great struggle poets of the preceding decades, one cannot fail to realise that despite all the obvious differences, there are a number of very important and very fundamental characteristics that are shared by virtually all these poems. Perhaps the most important of these is that they all have their roots in their poets' deeply-felt need to find a sense of equilibrium for themselves and for their community. Throughout the years of white minority rule, black South African poets have been concerned with a long and difficult search for the fulfilment of very simple but at the same time extremely fundamental human needs and values like 'fullness of life', 'respect' and a sense of belonging. It is these values and needs that Serote referred to when he talked about 'the simple things of life'. The biggest and most serious obstacle to the fulfilment of these basic needs was the institutionalised system of apartheid, a system that was especially designed to push a sizable segment of the South African nation into the gutters of society and deny them even the most fundamental and basic human rights. In other words, apartheid seriously disturbed an equilibrium that had been known and experienced by black South Africa before the arrival of the white settlers.

Throughout the history of black protest and resistance against white minority rule, black poets have been primarily concerned with attempting to regain this lost sense of equilibrium for themselves as well as their community. Initially, black South Africans could only regain some of the things they had been deprived of by starting a fierce and violent counter-offensive to meet the aggression of white South Africa. In those days, it was the poets' task to give spiritual guidance to that counter-offensive and to persuade the masses to give their physical and moral support to it.

However, now that part of the political imbalance has been addressed because of the political transformations of the early 1990s, the poets' role in society has transformed accordingly. They are no longer prepared to teach their community about guerrilla warfare or black pride, but have certainly not given up their 'consciousness-raising' efforts. In the new circumstances, there are important new challenges to meet. One part of the journey may have been completed, but the ultimate goal of equality, freedom, prosperity and justice for all has not yet been achieved. As long as political and social divisions remain, and as long as politicians and business leaders continue to be driven by greed and selfishness rather than by concern for the people, poets will continue to stand up and point out a different road ahead.

NOTES

1.   Steve Biko, *I Write What I Like* (London: Heinemann, 1978) 29.
2.   Kelwyn Sole, 'Oral Performance and Social Struggle in Contemporary Black South African Literature,' in *From South Africa: New Writings, Photographs, and Art*, eds David Bunn and Jane Taylor (Chicago: The University of Chicago Press, 1987) 256.
3.   Don Mattera, 'No Time, Black Man...' *Azanian Love Song* (Braamfontein: Skotaville, 1983) 46.
4.   James Matthews, 'Freedom's Child', *Cry Rage* (Johannesburg: SPRO-CAS, 1972) 68.
5.   Biko, 29.
6.   Dikobe wa Mogale, 'baptism of fire.' *baptism of fire* (Craighall: A.D. Donker, 1984) 10.
7.   Colin Gardner. 'The Poetry of Dikobe wa Mogale,' in *New Writing from Southern Africa*, ed. Emmanuel Ngara (London: James Currey, 1996), 158.
8.   Daniel P. Kunene, 'Language, Literature and the Struggle for Liberation in South Africa,' in *Perspectives on South African English Literature*, eds Michael Chapman et al (Parklands: AD. Donker, 1992) 498.
9.   Mongane Wally Serote, *Come and Hope With Me* (Claremont: David Philip, 1994) 12.
10. Seitlhamo Motsapi, 'the man', *earthstepper/the ocean is very shallow* (Grahamstown; Deep South Publishing, 1995) back cover.

Dramatic Excavations & Theatrical Explorations: Faustus, Ubu & Post-Apartheid South African Theatre

Michael Carklin

Helen: You are what you forget
            And the living feed on the dead
Gretchen: The hardest struggle is against forgetting
(Faustus in Africa, p.33).

The struggles and contradictions of memory and forgetting are challenges that confront South Africans daily as we continue to shake off the now rusty shackles of apartheid, to come to terms with the many horrifying and often moving stories revealed to us through the Truth and Reconciliation Commission, and as we move into a new century with new hope.[1] It is an engagement with the past that has been an imperative for many of our artists. I would argue that among the most exciting theatre to have been produced in South Africa during the last decade has been that which engages with the ambiguities and contradictions of the past through a critical confluence of sources. This chapter focuses on two examples of such work, *Faustus in Africa* and *Ubu and the Truth Commission* by William Kentridge and the Handspring Puppet Company. These are plays that seem to balk at simple messages. They challenge and confront the audience with confluences of imagery and style, with juxtapositions of actor and puppet, of three-dimensional stage action with two-dimensional animation.

In *Faustus in Africa*, the process of colonisation in Africa comes under close scrutiny as a Faustian explorer carves his way through the continent. *Ubu and the Truth Commission* utilises testimonies given at the Truth and Reconciliation Commission to present a poignant and thought-provoking multi-media perspective on the experience of accounting for past atrocities.

However, in utilising an eclectic and multi-layered synthesis of acting, puppetry, film, animation and music, these plays are unlike theatre works which offer theatrical histories or historically based stories that present us with fully constructed versions of the past. Rather, both *Faustus in Africa* and *Ubu and the Truth Commission* invite us, the audience, to participate more fully in the process of making meaning, of making sense of the past. They offer us narratives made up of fragments, clues, inter-textual references, and juxtaposed images, and it is thus the very nature of the theatre experience itself that offers us particular kinds of engagement with aspects of our past(s).

I will argue, therefore, that rather than understanding the work of these theatre-makers as being akin to that of the dramatic historian, it is perhaps more useful to understand it as a process of theatrical archeology in which we explore with them layers of imaginative debris, or excavate tangible fragments that could lead us to new insights into the manifold human experiences that constitute our past.

Probing memory through theatre

During the 1990s theatre practitioners in South Africa were faced with the challenge of re-appraising their role and approach. One of the primary concerns that emerged, both in the theatre and society more generally, has been a coming to terms with the past and an attempt to understand the various historical dynamics that have impacted on the present.[2] For example, the Truth and Reconciliation Commission, set up to investigate many of the atrocities committed during the apartheid era, has dominated much thinking in South Africa in recent years. It is this coming to terms with the past that has strongly influenced the ways in which South Africans engage with ideas of identity, history, heritage, language and place.

The writer of *Ubu and the Truth Commission*, Jane Taylor, suggests that it is the very process of 'Truth and Reconciliation' that influenced a shift in focus towards the personal narrative:

> Individual narratives come to stand for the larger national narrative. The stories of personal grief, loss, triumph and violation now stand as an account of South Africa's recent past. History and autobiography merge. This marks a significant shift, because in past decades of popular resistance, personal suffering was eclipsed – subordinated to a larger project of mass liberation.[3]

South African Nobel laureate, Nadine Gordimer, refers to Milan Kundera's injunction about the 'struggle of memory against forgetting',[4] when she suggests that there is a lot to write about now that apartheid is over. Given the slippery nature of memory and recollection, these processes of remembering are indeed struggles. However, in turning to the work of Kentridge and the Handspring Puppet Company, we see works that are not about *creating* memories, acting as theatrical reminders, or warning of the dangers of forgetting – rather, they are *interrogations* of such memories, critical comments on the ambiguous construction of the past.

As Kentridge himself states, 'our theatre is a reflection on the debate rather than the debate itself. It tries to make sense of the memory rather than be the memory'.[5] And in considering the notion of their theatre as a reflection on the debate, it is instructive to bear in mind Gary Gordon's comment that 'if the theatre provides a mirror of our world it should be more than a picture. It should also provide the opportunity for us to reflect on the reflection.'[6] For me, this is what makes the work of Kentridge and the Handspring Puppet Company so significant within the body of post-apartheid theatre in South Africa, for in a very tangible way it attempts to do just that.

Burdens of the past: Faustus and the burden of Europe; Ubu and the burden of Truth

In trying to 'make sense of the memory', the Company is acutely aware of the burdens of the past, and it is these burdens that seem to act as catalyst for many theatre makers. In the case of *Faustus in Africa*, it is the burden of Europe, in the case of *Ubu and the Truth Commission*, the heavy burdens of our more immediate past, and with these, the very burden of 'Truth' itself.

Director William Kentridge relates how he was given a two-volume translation of Goethe's *Faust* as Barmitzvah gift and how these stood unopened on his bookshelf for approximately twenty-five years silently rebuking him. Eventually, in the creating of *Faustus in Africa*, the company scoured a range of other versions of the story, including those of Christopher Marlowe, George Sand, Gertrude Stein and Bulgakov, but finally came back to Goethe's work, adding additional material by South African poet, Lesego Rampolokeng. Kentridge states:

> All this with the aim of finding the place where the play ceases to be the daunting other – the weight of Europe leaning on the Southern African tip of Africa – and becomes our own work.[7]

Significantly, in utilising a European work as the basis for this exploration, the Company do not try to identify themselves as 'an other' to Europe, but interrogate, and in so doing subvert, the very mythologies that have become so woven into the South African consciousness.

Where in Marlowe's *Dr Faustus*, we hear Faustus proclaiming that with the help of Mephistopheles

> I'll be great emperor of the world,
> And make a bridge through moving air
> To pass the ocean with a band of men;
> I'll join the hills that bind the Afric shore
> And make that country continent to Spain,
> And both contributory to my crown;[8]

in *Faustus in Africa*, we see Faustus as 'the explorer, cartographer, merchant, scholar, missionary, slaver',[9] attempting to do exactly that. It is in the pacts, the deals, the plans, and the actions of this Faustus that we can begin to make sense of our complex past.

The sense of critical reflection that is part of the process of this play, is revealed, however, in the acknowledgment that notions of History and Truth are so integrally linked to ideas of power.[10] It questions the very nature of history, memory and the documented past. In *Faustus in Africa*, Faustus' servant Johnston is bandaging the hyena (Mephisto's familiar), lamenting the fact that they are always the casualties while those with power tend to live in luxury:

> JOHNSTON: We stand outside the circle while they eat
> with the mud of our lives around our feet
> We look back to find we've left humanity behind
> We bury our pride and kneel so that our masters can ride.
>
>   ....
>
> I used to read a lot of History, to transport
> myself into the Spirit of the past
> To find out what great men have said and thought
> and see the glorious heights we've reached at last.
>
> HYENA: The spirit of the past? It's an empty crate,
> a rubbish dump where 'great men' can deposit
> the trash they make of their own generations.
> What's wrong?
> Never seen a dog talk? Cat got your tongue?
> *The Hyena laughs.*[11]

Whilst the weight of Europe may lie heavy on Southern Africa, its more immediate history brings with it the burden of truth, and, if not the lifting, then at least the replacing, for many, of the burden of guilt. The writer of *Ubu and the Truth Commission*, Jane Taylor, comments, however, that the play does not only explore a uniquely South African story: 'We in the late twentieth century live in an era of singular attention to questions of war crimes, reparations, global "peace-keeping". We are, it seems, increasingly aware of the obligation to hear testimony, even while we may yet be determining how to act upon what we have heard'.[12] But, as Lesley Marx so rightly points out, there is a paradox in a theatre of truth in an age of 'post structuralist anxiety'.[13]

Ubu and the Truth Commission is not a 'theatre of truth', but a theatre which interrogates the very idea of Truth. For Pa Ubu, a secret agent of the apartheid state responsible for many deaths, the burden is not between truths and lies (he is a master of deception after all), but between *concealing* and *revealing*, and it is precisely in what is revealed and how, that the problem of truth comes into focus. The theatre company is fully aware not only of the slipperiness of truth, but of the problems of a process which seeks the truth in order to effect reconciliation, as the following encounter between Pa Ubu and the puppet, Niles, a crocodile-cum-metaphorical-paper-shredder, reveals:

> Pa Ubu: Oh, Niles, such a vision I had. I saw the Great truth approaching, a rope in its hand. It demanded I speak the truth of our land.
> Niles: Well, as I understand things, you have a choice. You can take your chances, keep silent, and wait to see if the law comes after you. But once they have unmasked you, you'll have to face the music. My advice would be to pre-empt it all. I hear there is to be a Commission to determine Truths, Distortions and Proportions.
> Pa Ubu: I've heard of Truths, and know Distortions, but what are these Proportions you talk about?
> Niles: An enquiry is to be conducted by great and blameless men who measure what is done, and how, and why.
> Pa Ubu: And just what can these brilliant mathamunitions do?
> Niles: They can, beyond all ambiguity indicate when a vile act had a political purpose...[14]

This extract is by no means an attempt to undermine the very pain-filled testimonies given at the Truth and Reconciliation Commission or to make fun of the process itself, but it does alert us to the complexity of accounting for actions of the past. The notion of 'blameless men' judging 'beyond all ambiguity' whether an act of violence was political or not throws into question the very processes we use to try and discover 'truths'.

Further in the play when Pa Ubu is confronted by a large Ubu shadow puppet (his conscience perhaps?), Pa Ubu realises that there is another option besides 'conceal or reveal'. The Shadow says 'I have another suggestion: shift the burden of guilt. Take the initiative; find a name, and remove yourself from all trace of blame. *Extract yourself from the plot of your own history.*' To which Pa Ubu replies: 'We have nothing to be ashamed of. We were only doing our job!'[15] Immediately following this statement a witness gives further testimony of how his son was killed by having his head hit repeatedly against a wall, providing a stark juxtaposition to Ubu's own deliberations.

Kentridge is well aware of the danger of trivialising or doing an injustice to the material drawn from the Truth and Reconciliation Commission, and in questioning how we can do honour to such material, suggests that as far as he has a polemic it is this: 'to trust in the inauthentic, the contingent, the practical as a way of arriving at meaning'.[16] The juxtaposing of Jarryesque burlesque with transcripts from real testimony given at the Truth and Reconciliation Commission provides a somewhat unsettling experience for the audience. We both laugh and are horrified, and as Taylor argues, through our laughter we also become implicated. The stark juxtaposition of the slapstick comic and the extremely serious is, however, a crucial way through which the Company gives expression to the past. If, as Taylor suggests, Cause and Effect are registered through different modes of expression in the play, the resulting performance aesthetic is ultimately not one of the theatre as escapist arena or comfort zone, but one in which it becomes an extremely disjunctive, yet powerful, confrontation between past and present, between decision and consequence.

This suggests then that the past is constituted of multiple narratives and diverse experiences, but that additionally, it consists of those narratives that are never told, perhaps through secrecy, perhaps through marginalisation. This then brings us back to my idea of theatrical archeology and the possibilities for theatre to probe such a past.

Theatrical archaeology

The play as a form of theatrical archaeology suggests a particular kind of relationship to the past, one that is aware of its vastness, its ambiguities, its secrets. It gives us a chance to turn the soil, to excavate layers, perhaps to encounter new voices or silenced voices.

I would suggest that it is in the theatrical juxtapositions that this approach to theatre-making is clearest: the juxtapositions between image and word and action, between puppet and actor, between cryptic clue and linear narrative, between past and present. In *Faustus in Africa*, two particularly good examples are the pact between Faustus and Mephisto, and the Banquet scene in which Faustus is seen to literally carve up Africa. Faustus and Mephisto make a wager, and Faustus is required to sign in blood. The stage directions read:

> Mephisto takes Faustus' arm. On the screen a mosquito lands on a naked arm, transforms into a hypodermic syringe, sucks up a blood sample, transforms back into a mosquito and flies off. The mosquito lands on the document. A stamp descends annihilating the insect. The stamp lifts to reveal Faustus' signature.[17]

Similarly, when Faustus is feasting:

> Faustus eats as Mephistopheles and an office worker put plates in front of him. On the screen: Silver salvers corresponding to the dishes brought on stage. The plates of food are a grapefruit that becomes a mine. A slave ship that becomes an ocean liner. A forest that is cut down. A village that becomes a hotel. A map that gets cut in four. And an overflowing water reservoir.[18]

For me this is a particularly good example of the way that theatre is working to subvert the content it is drawing on. The animation juxtaposed with word and action is not simply historical representation – rather, it becomes the ironic presentation of aspects of the past. Familiar images and motifs are placed in relation to one another to suggest a complexity of historical sub-texts.

We see a similar use of image and action in *Ubu and the Truth Commission*.

Pa Ubu switches on a light. He is to one side of the stage in the glass booth which is used as a shower. Ma Ubu lies in her armchair. A soft spotlight comes on to show Pa Ubu in the shower.[19]

The animated images that we see on the screen while Pa is singing in the shower are of body parts, blood, human remains washing down the plug hole. He is cleansing himself of his deeds. Significantly, in the very next scene, the glass booth becomes a translation booth for the translator at the Truth and Reconciliation Commission hearings, and tellingly, the caption on the screen which reads 'A Bath' quickly morphs to 'A Bloodbath'.[20]

It is these fragments of history that become evidence to the past. And it is often those fragments that are hidden, silenced, or buried – removed from official histories – that are excavated and pieced together to reveal alternative stories of the past, thus highlighting the very incompleteness of the idea of History itself. These are the bits that are not so easily digested, those non-biodegradable fragments of history that come back in evidence. As we see in the play:

Pa Ubu grabs Niles and begins to stuff documents down his throat. In the intervals, while Pa Ubu retrieves more pieces, Niles interjects.
Niles: What's this I taste?
A bit of skull shattered in pieces,
A pair of hands torn off at the wrists,
Some poisoned scalps shorn of their fleeces,
Some half-burned skin injected with cysts.

As they say, *fiat experimentum in corpore vili*, that is, let experiment be made on a worthless body. But there are some tougher bits, not so easily digested.
A piece of tongue that would not be silent,
A beaten back that ignored the ache,
A hand up-raised in gesture defiant,
A blood-red heart that would not break....[21]

Giving voice

This process of 'theatrical archaeology' is not only about revealing objects, images, artefacts, or clues. Perhaps most significantly it is about plumbing the depths to hear echoes of voices of the past – to literally give voice where previously we have encountered silence.

Where earlier we have seen Johnston and the Hyena discussing the 'great men' of history, we now hear the voices of Gretchen and of Helen of Troy, a further indication of the play's critical engagement. Perhaps one of the best known descriptions of Helen comes in Marlowe's *Dr Faustus*:

Was this the face that launch'd a thousand ships
And burnt the topless towers of Ilium?
Sweet Helen, make me immortal with a kiss.
Her lips suck forth my soul: see where it flies![22]

Where previously she is only a vision, she is now given voice:

> I, Helen, much admired and much abused have come from yonder shore, where
> lately we disembarked still giddy from the restless rocking of the seas.
>
> I have seen many and terrible happenings
> Warfare and anguish, night in the city.
> Did I see this or did I imagine what my fear called up....
>
> I've run tracks through time
> Been through the writings of history
> With predators always at my back and all around.[23]

And, as Helen later tells the hyena:

> Desirability has proved my liability....[24]

The contradictions of Helen's position – as historical figure, mythical
person, and literary and theatrical symbol – become clear. Is she the image
of perfection that many strive for (as Marlowe's image suggests) or does she
become the ultimate scapegoat? Significantly, I would argue, the words
that the playwright ascribes to Helen are not unambivalent reflections,
but insights which call into question her very own position in history and
literature, which question her own marginalisation and exploitation.

Conclusions, confluences, fusions, and con-fusions

As the archaeologist digs through layers, dusts off shards, and pieces
together fragments, he or she encounters a confluence (or divergence) of
time, space, knowledge, prediction and imagination. In this sense, these
plays, in drawing on Goethe's *Faust* and Jarry's *Ubu* plays, become confluences of sources, ideas and concerns. Such theatrical confluence is an
important aspect of postcolonial artistic expression, and in a context of
unprecedented global communication, one cannot but consider notions
of cultural meetings, confluences, hybrids, fusions, and/or syncretic
forms of expression. From Peter Brook's contentious version of *The
Mahabharata* to Eugenio Barba's excursions into Africa for cultural barter,
and from Mbongeni Ngema, Percy Mtwa and Barney Simon's *Woza
Albert!* to Femi Osofisan's *The Oriki of a Grasshopper* to the contemporary adaptation of *Romeo and Juliet* for film, we see, albeit in different
ways, a need to extend beyond the boundaries of one's own immediate
environment, to understand one's identity, perhaps not in opposition to
the other, but in light of the many experiences of others. The question that
is posed, however, is what form such confluence takes and what power
relations are implied in such meetings.[25]

In South Africa, such confluence takes on different forms, from what
might be called an aesthetics of 'fusion', which, at its crudest, suggests

that the stirring of a variety of cultural ingredients into a melting pot, decorated with a liberal sprinkling of 'ethnic' spice, will result in a feast of New South African Culture (with a capital C), to a more critical engagement with a myriad of sources and ideas. In this light, I would argue strongly that rather than being seen as 'Africanisations' or 'modernisations' of European plays, both *Faustus in Africa* and *Ubu and the Truth Commission* engage with themes in such a way that they avoid becoming 'fusion' plays; rather they are clearly articulated original South African statements. In other words, they are able to resist the seductive trend prevalent among some South African artists, to work towards a blend of European and African aesthetics to produce a form of 'Rainbow Nation aesthetics', which, I would suggest, very seldom probes beneath the surface to the complex hearts of its component parts. In a sense, perhaps, they are deliberate theatrical 'con-fusions'

Rather than working toward composite messages, their approach increases the challenge for the negotiation of meaning and pushes the boundaries of theatrical communication. We should bear in mind Susan Sontag's statement from *Against Interpretation* that 'What is important now is to recover our senses. We must learn to see more, to hear more, to feel more.'[26] It is these shifting boundaries that one experiences when watching the play, that would support the writer's comment that 'there is thus, I suppose, a sense of ambiguity produced by the play. This is not an ambiguity about the experience of loss and pain suffered; rather it is an ambiguity about how we respond to such suffering.'[27] Arguably, this is part of the challenge that much theatre in South Africa now challenges the audience with – not simply complex views of past experiences, but with ambivalence which makes the individual stories of so many others our stories too.

NOTES

1. The Truth and Reconciliation Commission (TRC) was the body that operated under the chairpersonship of Archbishop Desmond Tutu, conducting hearings into political acts of violence during the apartheid era, and considering requests for amnesty from both agents of the state and members of liberation movements. I would argue that the looking towards the future with new hope was perhaps best seen in the vision of South African President Thabo Mbeki, of an 'African Renaissance' and his continued insistence that the 21st century should be the 'African Century'.
2. Breyten Breytenbach, *Johnny Cockroach* (unpublished, first presented July 1999); Greig Coetzee, *White Man with Weapons* (unpublished, first performed 1996); Paul Herztberg, *The Dead Wait* (unpublished; first performed 1997); Phyllis Kotz, 'Isizwe Sethu: Our Nation' (Small Ndaba and the Sibikwa Players, first presented 1999); Dumo kaNdlovu, *The Game* (unpublished, first performed 1997); Deon Opperman, *Donkerland* (Cape Town: Tafelberg, 1996); Chris Pretorius, *Dark Continent* (unpublished, first performed July 1999); Lesogo Rampolokeng, *The Story I am About to Tell: Indaba Engizoyixoxa* (unpublished; first performed July 1999).
3. Taylor 2.

4. Cathy Maree, 'Resistance and Remembrance: Theatre During and After Dictatorship and Apartheid', *South African Theatre Journal*, 12, 1 & 2 (1998): 21.
5. Kentridge in Taylor ix.
6. Gordon 92.
7. Kentridge, Programme: *Faustus in Africa*, no page numbering.
8. Marlowe 22–3.
9. *Faustus in Africa* 1.
10. In *Power/Knowledge*, Foucault argues that 'truth isn't outside power ... it is produced only by virtue of multiple forms of constraint.... "Truth" is to be understood as a system of ordered procedures for the production, regulation, distribution, circulation and operation of statements' (p.133). We should also note Hayden White's argument that 'once it is admitted that all histories are in some sense interpretations, it becomes necessary to determine the extent to which historians' explanations of past events can qualify as objective, if not rigorously scientific, accounts of reality' (p.51).
11. *Faustus in Africa* 14.
12. Taylor vii.
13. Marx 213.
14. Taylor 17.
15. Taylor 55. Emphasis mine.
16. Kentridge in Taylor xi.
17. *Faustus in Africa* 8.
18. *Faustus in Africa* 29.
19. Taylor 9.
20. Taylor 11.
21. Taylor 33/35.
22. Marlowe 92.
23. *Faustus in Africa* 24.
24. *Faustus in Africa* 27.
25. The late twentieth century has seen the opening of much debate regarding the sharing, borrowing, and often 'stealing' of forms of theatrical expression across cultures, particularly regarding the appropriation of African and Indian dramatic forms by theatre exponents in the west. It is therefore imperative that we are critically cautious in attempting to understand the kinds of artistic and political dynamics that underpin theatrical confluence.
26. Sontag 14.
27. Taylor v.

WORKS CITED

Carrière, Jean-Claude, *The Mhabharata: A play based on the Indian classic epic*, trans. Peter Brook. Production directed by Peter Brook, London: Methuen, 1987.
Foucault, Michel, *Power/Knowledge: Selected Interviews and Other Writings*, ed. Colin Gordon, New York: Harvester Wheatsheaf, 1980.
Goethe, Johann Wolfgang, *Faust: Part 1*, trans. Bayard Taylor, rev. and ed. Stuart Atkins, New York: Collier Books, 1962.
Gordon, Gary, 'Lessons and Mirrors: steps to consider in the education of the dance maker' in *Confluences: Cross-Cultural Fusions in Music and Dance*. Proceedings of the first South African Music and Dance Conference, 16–19 July 1997, Cape Town: University of Cape Town, 1997.
Kentridge, William, and the Handspring Puppet Company, *Faustus in Africa*, Unpublished manuscript.
—— and the Handspring Puppet Company, *Programme: Faustus in Africa*, Johannesburg: Mannie Manim Productions and the Market Theatre Company, 1995.
—— and the Handspring Puppet Company, *Programme: Ubu & the Truth Commission*, Johannesburg: Mannie Manim Productions and the Market Theatre Company, 1997.
Maree, Cathy, 'Resistance and Remembrance: Theatre during and after dictatorship and apartheid', *South African Theatre Journal*, 12, 1 & 2, 1998: 11–33.
Marlowe, Christopher, *The Tragical History of the Life and Death of Doctor Faustus*, ed. John D.

Jump, London: Methuen, 1962.

Marx, Lesley, 'Slouching Towards Bethlehem: *Ubu and the Truth Commission*', *African Studies* 57, 2, 1998: 209–20.

Mtwa, Percy, Mbongeni Ngema, and Barney Simon, *Woza Albert!* London: Methuen, 1983.

Osofisan, Femi, *The Oriki of a Grasshopper and Other Plays*, Washington DC: Howard University Press, 1995.

Sontag, Susan, *Against Interpretation*, New York: Dell Publishers, 1966.

Taylor, Jane, *Ubu and the Truth Commission*, Cape Town: University of Cape Town Press, 1988.

White, Hayden, *Tropics of Discourse: Essays in Cultural Criticism*, Baltimore and London: Johns Hopkins University Press, 1978.

FILMOGRAPHY

Kentridge, William, and the Handspring Puppet Company, *Faustus in Africa*: Extracts for Publicity Material. 1995. Supplied by Mannie Manim Productions.

Kentridge, William, and the Handspring Puppet Company, *Ubu & the Truth Commission*: Extracts for Publicity Material. 1997. Supplied by Mannie Manim Productions.

William Shakespeare's Romeo & Juliet, directed by Baz Luhrmann. Screenplay by Baz Luhrmann and Craig Pearle, based on play by William Shakespeare. USA, 1996.

The Stereotyping of Whites
in Xhosa Prose Fiction

C. R. Botha

Introduction

The aim of this article is to investigate the transcultural nature of Xhosa prose fiction. Within the context of literature, transculturalism may be defined as the depiction of members of alternative language groups in the text, in addition to the depiction of members of the target group, by an author who is also a member of the latter group. As this topic has not been dealt with adequately in the past this study can only be regarded as a preliminary investigation which, it is hoped, will stimulate further research.

Every literary text, insofar as it aspires to be of literary significance, contains some form of comment on the universal aspects of human life and values. Within the southern African context, the mutual relationships between the various language groups form an important part of this reality. A transcultural study is one which is specifically aimed at the study of these relationships. Such a study is normally based quite firmly on socio-literary principles, as it seeks to examine literature within a particular sociological context. The validity of such an approach is acknowledged by White and Couzens (1984:1) when they state:

> Although literature and literary criticism have a strong momentum of their own, they can never be autonomous activities.... The criticism of literature, in short, has everything to do with the criticism of society.

The sociological importance of a study of this nature is also acknowledged by Sarah Milbury-Steen (1980: ix) when she introduces her own study on transculturalism by saying: 'In it nonliterary factors have been weighed quite heavily, for cross-cultural perception is basically a historical, psychological and sociological process.'

The study of literature from a socio-literary viewpoint could be of particular relevance to the southern African region. There can be no doubt about the fact that this region is culturally and linguistically diverse. The southernmost tip of Africa has, over the years, evolved into a place of encounter for people of various origins, such as the West, Asia and Africa.

For many reasons, this encounter soon developed into an escalating form of tension and conflict. Swanepoel (1987:60) puts it as follows:

> Intergroup contact, whenever it started, has been a major cause of instability. Flux and instability have given rise to tension and conflict from the seventeenth century to this day – between San and Khoi, African and African, Dutch and Khoi, African and San, Afrikaner and African, African and English, Afrikaner and English, black and white, and various others.

Inevitably the result of this process was a growing tendency towards isolationism between these respective groups which on its part led to the development of a wide range of mutual misperceptions amongst them. Mphahlele, as quoted by Malan (1987:4), quite aptly states:

> For many years whites knew people of a different skin colour only as enemies on the battlefield or as slaves or servants, or porters on expeditions ... the missionaries who came to know the coloured people a little better regarded them as proselytes or potential proselytes, but still saw them as members of a group whose heathen culture had to be eradicated ... the free burghers, Voortrekkers, and even the British Settlers were regarded by blacks as conquerors in the name of Christianity.

The tendency towards isolationism also had a profound effect on the literature of this region. Over the years a number of separate literary traditions were born, all of which existed in a state of growing isolationism from one another. This situation has prompted critics such as White and Couzens (1984:1) to ask questions such as the following:

> Is there, then ... a single South African literature? Are there not at least five literatures operating alongside each other, each with its own traditions and conventions, even its own audience, and achieving only the most rudimentary of contacts and mutual influences?

It is important that this tendency towards isolationism in literature should be addressed and counteracted as effectively as possible. Every work should reflect, to a greater or lesser degree, 'the interactions between peoples of diverse origins, languages, technologies and social systems meeting on South African soil' (White and Couzens 1984:1). Authors should make it their duty to experiment with the theme of transculturalism by investigating the cultural diversity of the region in a critical manner. By following this route, the author would help to combat the growth of mutual misperceptions which tend to destroy society.

In spite of this strong tendency towards isolationism in the South African literary tradition, some experimentation within the field of transculturalism has, in fact, already taken place in the various literatures of the region. In Sotho literature, for example, an author such as Nqheku has depicted this theme successfully in his novel *Arola naheng ya Maburu* (1942). In the Zulu novel *Nigabe Ngani?* (Zuma 1965), this theme is also explored successfully. In the paragraphs below we will now attempt to establish how, and to what extent, this theme is pursued more specifically in Xhosa prose fiction.

Transculturalism in Xhosa prose fiction

Method of study
This investigation seeks to address the role of the transcultural theme in Xhosa prose fiction. It wishes to establish whether the texts which form part of this genre are mainly homogenous in nature, or whether the respective African authors also reveal a significant degree of sensitivity to distinguish between, for example, the Afro-European or the Afro-Asiatic in the South African context.

For practical reasons, this chapter is limited to a study of only a small portion of this particular field. Priority will be given to the depiction of whites in Xhosa prose fiction, and to the Xhosa author's perception of the role played by this particular community in the past. This is due primarily to the fact that socio-cultural interaction in the South African region has, over the years, taken place mainly between black and white. Swanepoel (1987: 60), for instance, says the following in this regard:

> Most topical as far as inter-group conflict is concerned, is the one that has become associated, paradoxically, with the colour of the skin. *Black* and *White* have become symbols of opposing forces ... For creative writing in Southern Africa, this has provided multiple avenues for *Rohstoff.*

This, however, does not mean that other non-African groups, such as the so-called 'Coloureds' and Afro-Asians, do not also play a most important and relevant role in Xhosa prose fiction.

This article forms part of an envisaged comprehensive study on Xhosa prose fiction. The aim of the study is to analyse the role of transculturalism in this genre since its inception in 1823 up to the present. Such a study, which might cast valuable light on the development of social relations between Africans and non-Africans over the decades could, for study purposes, be subdivided into the following phases:

1   1823–1900
2   1901–1945
3   1946–present.

Whilst most of the literary data pertaining to the last two phases is quite readily accessible in places such as academic libraries, that pertaining to the first phase is more problematic. The reason for this lies in the rather unconventional mode of existence of this data in the form of early narratives which appeared randomly in magazines, newspapers, etc. Literary material of this nature is often located in places other than academic libraries (eg. state archives and church libraries) both locally and abroad. The study of this phase would consequently require a research methodology which is not only quite specialised, but also quite different from that required for the study of the remaining two phases. For this reason an unconventional research strategy will have to be followed whereby the last two phases are studied first and the experience gained in this manner is then (where applicable) used in the future analysis of phase 1. In light, however, of the severe restrictions on the length of articles submitted for publication in most scientific journals, only *one* of the phases mentioned above can be analysed here. This article, therefore, will only concentrate on the most important novels published during the first four decades of the twentieth century, up to 1945.

It is clear that the relationships between black and white, as they are known today, were largely forged during the period between 1901 and 1945. Whilst, on the one hand, this can be regarded as the period during which the process of colonial imperialism had reached its peak, it may also be regarded as the period of awakening of African nationalism, as is witnessed by the establishment of the ANC in 1912, and subsequent events. We believe that a critical study of black perceptions regarding white people during this particular period could go a long way in helping us to understand some of the events South Africans are experiencing today on the socio-political front.

The role of the white stereotype in Xhosa prose fiction

This investigation into the texts from this particular period has revealed that the transcultural theme is not actively pursued by some of the authors from this period. A text such as Mqhayi's *Ityala lamawele* (1981), for instance, concentrates mainly on important aspects of African tradition and custom. In *UMqhayi waseNtabozuko* ([1939] 1964) the author's consciousness of the white man/woman is limited to general references to the Western socio-political system, where whites are depicted as typical opportunists who tend to exploit the African:

> Imvisiswano kuthi ayikho;
> sisezisisulu zeentshaba zethu,
> Uyazenzela umfo oMhlophe;
> athabathe omnye
> abethe abanye ngaye;
> (Mqhayi 1981: 67)

> There is no unity amongst us, we are still
> an easy prey for our enemies. The white
> man does as he likes. He takes one person
> and uses him against another.

It seems in particular as if the authors who belong to the earlier years of this period of study, are not conscious enough of the white man's role (whether positive or negative) in the South African context. Sinxo, for instance, pays little attention to whites in his first two novels, *UNomsa* (1922) and *Umfundisi waseMtuqwasi* (1927). In these novels the author concentrates mainly on his leading characters of African origin, to the extent that the theme of transculturalism is granted only a marginal role.

The heterogeneous nature of the South African population, therefore, does not receive much recognition in these early texts. In spite of the rather negative tendency outlined above, not all the works from this period should be regarded as totally apathetic. The later authors from this period generally seem to be more conscious of inter-group relations and a variety of cross-cultural references are, in fact, to be found in some of the texts under discussion. For the purposes of this article, these references are grouped into two separate categories, each of which will now be discussed individually in the paragraphs below.

In some of the works from this period, cross-cultural references firstly manifest themselves in the form of general references to the Western socio-political system. The white man's role as defender and upholder of this system within the South African context is frequently referred to. Some of these references are quite positive in nature and reflect a healthy relationship on the cross-cultural level. During the description of the wedding ceremony in *Ingqumbo Yeminyanya* (Jordan, [1940] 1980: 143) for instance, the narrator acknowledges the keen support given to this ceremony by the white friends of the wedding couple.

Cross-cultural references of a more negative kind, however, are also to be found in this novel of Jordan's. The British Government's annexation of the Transkeian Territories towards the end of the previous century seems to be a matter of particular concern to this author. The unfair treatment meted out to blacks by the Westerner in their country of birth consequently receives frequent attention. During the early phases of the story, for instance, reference is made to the British Government's repeated attempts to confiscate the land of the Xhosa. The Xhosa's resistance to these attempts is firmly entrenched in their folk narratives. One of these narratives, as presented by Ngxabane, partially reads as follows:

> *Unangoku ke abeLungu mhla bamvingcela uMhlontlo emqolombeni ngem-*
> *fazwse kaHophu baba ngasuka bejolisa bedubula batsho phantsi. UMhlonrlo*
> *wayexhagwe zizinja ezimbini, zingaziwa ukuba zivela phi na, zizinqaga*
> *ziziginya zonke ezo mbumbulwana zabeLungu.*   (Jordan, 1980: 9)

When, during the Hope war, the white soldiers surrounded Mhlontlo in a cave and aimed their rifles at him several times, they failed to kill him. Mhlontlo was guarded by two dogs but nobody knew where they came from. They caught and swallowed those small bullets of the white people.

The white man's lack of understanding and sensitivity regarding the fundamental cultural values of the Xhosa is another matter of great concern to Jordan. During the earlier phases of his novel, for instance, mention is made of a meeting between the Bishop, Gcinizibele and Zwelinzima. The narrator says the following:

> *iBishophu yayise ilenzile idinga noGcinizibele. AbaPhesheya ke bona abantu*
> *abalindikubuzwa mvelaphi xa baziyo ukuba uyaziwa umcimbi abawuhambe-*
> *leyo. IBhisophu ke ngako oko yathi ifika yabe isithi gca ingena emcimbini. ...*

Ngokubazi ke abantu abaMhlophe uGcinizibele wakhawulezisa ukucinga.
(Jordan, 1980: 45–6)

The Bishop had already made an appointment with Gcinizibele. Westerners do not wait to complete formalities regarding the reason for their visit when it is already known. The Bishop opened up the discussion immediately.... Gcinizibele knew the customs of the white people and therefore did not object to this.

The white man's apparent lack of consideration for African protocol is clearly illustrated here by Jordan. Even the Bishop, who is known for his kindness towards blacks, does not seem to have the necessary understanding of the black man's protocol. Gcinizibele's reaction, on the other hand, shows that he has already come to accept, to a large extent, the fact that the Westerner is unable to understand the African value system. Should he wish to negotiate successfully with the Westerner, it would be wise for him not to cling too tightly to his own procedures or protocol.

In his work *Umzali Wolahleko* ([1933] 1973) Sinxo also makes frequent reference to the Western socio-political system. The representatives of this system are often criticised for showing a negative attitude towards blacks. In one instance, for example, the reader is informed about a faction fight between two groups of youths in the rural areas of former Ciskei. Some of the youths are arrested and brought to trial. The case is heard by a white magistrate, who sentences each of the youths to a period of three months in jail or a fine of thirty Rand. The narrator comments as follows on this relatively light sentence:

AbeLungu sebesuka basenze sincinci isigwebo setyala elilolu hlobo, ngokun-gathi bathi, 'Ziyekeni iimfene zigqibane xa zizibulala ngokwazo'.
(Sinxo 1973: 27)

White people are inclined to issue a light penalty in cases such as these, as if they wish to say: 'Leave the baboons alone, let them finish one another off themselves if they wish to.'

Apart from these general references to the Western system, the trans-cultural theme also manifests itself in the depiction of individual members of the white community. An author such as Mqhayi, for instance, pays keen attention to white characters in his novel *UDon Jadu* ([1928] n.d.). During one of his travels, the main character (Don Jadu) is confronted by three white horsemen. These 'amaBhulu' (Afrikaners) accuse him of trespassing on their property. He is forcefully escorted to the entrance of the farm and addressed harshly in a most insulting and degrading manner:

Usibhadam sesidalwa! Siyatha semfene! Sidenge soKafile!   (Mqhayi n.d.:13)

You idiot! Ignorant baboon! Stupid Kaffir!

Don Jadu is thereafter assaulted with a whip. When a group of black people unexpectedly appear on the scene, the white men are shown to flee in a most cowardly manner. In this scene, the Westerner (and specifically the

Afrikaner) is depicted in a most negative manner as a violent bully. The Afrikaner is a caricature who is stereotyped as a coward fleeing from the scene whenever he encounters the slightest form of resistance.

In the ensuing scene, however, Don Jadu visits the home of another white family in order to obtain some food. He is received in a most cordial and hospitable manner by this Afrikaner family, who invite him to enter and to make himself at home. He is offered enough food and drink and the family take a keen interest in his wellbeing. Don Jadu is particularly impressed with the family's strong sense of religion (Mqhayi n.d.: 17–19).

This episode is most functional in the novel, as it largely contradicts the one involving the horsemen. The initial stereotyping of the Afrikaner as a bully and a racist is in strong contrast with this last scene. By this juxtaposition, the narrator wishes to confirm the universal principle which applies to all nations and communities, namely that each group of people possesses cruel and wicked, as well as good and kind elements. Mqhayi summarises the position by saying:

> ... *amaBhulu ke ngabona bantu banconywayo ngokungamfuni umntu omnyama, nokumcekisa; ... Kwiintlanga ezimhlophe, ezingengawo amaBhulu ngelo xesha kwakukho intetho esetyenziswayo ethi: 'Ubom bomntu omnyama, bunganeno kobenciniba, nobenja yomLungu.' Eli Bhulu lide layidubula inja yalo ngenxa yomnyama, ingamtyanga nokumtya. Le nto ifundisa ukuba akukho sizwe sisisikhohlakali ngendalo; bakho abangabantu nabangebantu kuzo zonke iintlanga.*   (Mqhayi n.d.: 19)

> Afrikaners are known for their hatred of the black man.... Amongst the white nations, not including the Afrikaners, there was the following expression: 'The life of a black man has less value than that of an ostrich, or that of the dog of a white man.' This Afrikaner was prepared to kill his dog in the interests of a black man. This shows us that there is no nation which is evil in nature – there are those who are human and those who are inhuman amongst all nations.

Another author from this period who experiments quite extensively with the transcultural theme is Jordan. In his novel *Ingqumbo Yemi-nyanya* (1980), white characters feature more prominently and his tran-scultural references are more innovative in the sense that they include white males (to be discussed below) as well as white females such as the Matron (p. 42) and Sister Monica (p. 120). Particular reference is made to the role of the white cleric in the African community. During the earlier phases of the story, reference is made to the important role of the white Bishop as a guide and counsellor to a relatively young and inexperienced Zwelinzima at Fort Hare University. The Bishop is depicted as a person with a sound understanding of the African mind. He says to Zwelinzima:

> *Mntwan'am, nokondimblophenje, abantu abaNtsundu ndibleli kakhulu nabo, ndaye ndinamasiko endi wancomayo kubo.*   (Jordan 1980:38)

> My son, although I am white, I have a lot of knowledge about Africans and I have great respect for their traditions.

The Bishop is presented as a positive stereotype in the novel. The emphasis is generally upon his idiosyncrasies as a man of religion, rather than upon his particular personal features as a human being. He possesses all the features which are typical of his profession. He is educated, patient and understanding. Characterisation is therefore limited to the portrayal of only a narrow spectrum of superficial, typical features. Malan (1987: 4) quite aptly says the following in this regard:

> Earlier literary works of most languages portray the missionary in the role of helper; thus a religious and educational mentor. They have also made the greatest contribution to the establishing of written African literatures. Although the missionaries were praised by the writers in African languages, ... they were also strongly criticised.

The second white character who features prominently in the story is also a missionary. He is Father Williams, the head of St Cuthbert's Mission in Transkei. After his departure for Mpondomiseland, Zwelinzima builds up a close friendship with the missionary, who is portrayed as a friendly and sympathetic person. The function of guide and counsellor, which originally belonged to the Bishop, now becomes that of Father Williams.

The divergent conduct of the new chief and his wife in Mpondomiseland soon leads to the development of widespread dissatisfaction amongst his followers. Father Williams decides to visit the village of Jenca in order to defuse local tensions. He is accompanied by one of his loyal supporters, Ngubengwe. On their arrival at Jenca, Ngubengwe informs the missionary that the people are singing war songs and that they should not enter the village owing to the hostile atmosphere. The missionary, however, replies that he regards this as only a normal, everyday song and that they should have nothing to fear (Jordan, 1980: 210). Shortly afterwards, the visitors are approached by a group of youths who ask them for tobacco. Ngubengwe immediately recognises this as another act of hostility, as it is improper to beg for tobacco from a cleric. Father Williams, however, does not agree with him. To him, the exchange of tobacco is an old and highly-respected African custom. He criticises Ngubengwe for acting so suspiciously towards the people of Jenca. Shortly afterwards a vicious attack is launched on the visitors. Ngubengwe is killed instantly, whilst Father Williams is saved from certain death by one of the local people.

Through his presentation of the tragic events at Jenca, Jordan wishes to emphasise an important matter concerning cross-cultural relationships. These events are intended to draw our attention to the fact that it will never be possible for the white man to come to a full understanding of the African mind. The Westerner can only, at best, have a superficial knowledge of his/her black compatriots. Had Father Williams paid more attention to the warnings of Ngubengwe, a most tragic incident could have been averted. Instead, he chose to depend on his own limited perceptions of the African mind, with disastrous consequences.

In *Ingqumbo Yeminyanya* (Jordan 1980) the white man is stereotyped as someone who tends to overestimate his knowledge and understanding of the African. The narrator hereby confirms a notion which is recurrent and basic to this novel, that is, the inaccessibility of black culture and thought to the outsider. As a cultural foreigner, the white man can, at best, possess only a superficial knowledge of Africans. That is why a person such as Father Williams comes to the conclusion that:

> *wathi ebesithi uyamqonda umntu oNtsundu waziqonda loo mini ukuba akokamazi konke. Waphindela eNgcolosi ejingisa intloko kukudana.*
> (Jordan 1980: 207)

> He who thought that he understood the African realised that day that he did not understand him at all. He returned to St Cuthberts a disappointed man.

Conclusion

This brief investigation of early Xhosa prose fiction has revealed that the transcultural theme has not been developed adequately in the novels examined. The emphasis is mainly on the portrayal of aspects of the dominant culture, whilst the depiction of related cultural groups is, to a large degree, neglected. The works under discussion, therefore, do not provide a clear picture of the Xhosa's perception of the Westerner during this particular period. A limited degree of attention is, however, given to the Westerner in some later instances and there do seem to be promising signs of progress in the depiction of this theme. In most of these works, the characters are one-dimensional, stereotypical figures who are portrayed in strict accordance with certain basic traits. Meaningful integration of both positive *and* negative personal features in a single character on a more complex level is seldom found.

It is, however, important to consider the tendencies outlined above in their proper perspective. It is evident that similar tendencies are to be found in other literary traditions from this period. The first demerit mentioned here, namely the tendency towards cultural isolation and a general lack of transcultural consciousness, also seems to form an integral part of English and Afrikaans prose fiction during this period. From 1901 to 1945 the tendency towards cultural isolationism in the southern African context was quite severe. This phenomenon affected most facets of social life in the region, including literature. Authors who belonged to a particular language group were often reluctant to pay attention to members of other groups in their works and concentrated largely on the depiction of members of their own cultural group. Mphahlele (1987: 48) puts it as follows: 'There is a formidable wall between black and white, and there is hardly any opportunity to get to know one another intimately. We seem to be looking at each other through a small opening in the wall between us.'

As a result, the first depiction of the black man on a substantial and significant level in South African English prose fiction only took place at a relatively late stage during this particular period. The first widely read imaginative works exploring the cross-cultural theme were only written in the late 1920s by authors such as William Plomer and Sarah Gertrude Millin. In Plomer's *Turbott Wolfe* (1926), for instance, the sexual relationship between a couple who are members of opposite race groups is depicted in an elaborate and sympathetic manner, thereby introducing the transcultural theme into this particular literary tradition.

The first significant treatment of the transcultural theme in Afrikaans literature occurred comparatively late – in 1931 – with the publication of *Booia* (Jochem van Bruggen). This was followed by the fiction of P. J. Schoeman during the 1940s which concentrated on the depiction of the Swazi (for example, *Mboza die Swazi en ander verhale*, 1941) as well as F. A. Venter's *Swart Pelgrim* (1952) which portrayed the Xhosa. Transcultural depiction, therefore, only entered Afrikaans prose fiction at a relatively late stage and Afrikaans authors were mostly pre-occupied with the portrayal of characters who form part of their own language group. Thus Malan (1987:3) rightly concludes that:

> It was mainly during the second half of the twentieth century that writers began to examine the problem of inter-ethnic relationships which had previously received little attention in literature.

The tendency towards monoculturalism which has been identified in this study, therefore, seems not to be limited to Xhosa prose fiction only, but also appears to be present in other literary traditions from this period.

In spite of the general tendency outlined above, a limited degree of experimentation with the transcultural theme was identified in some of the later novels between 1901 and 1945. Authors such as Sinxo and Jordan seem to be more conscious of the multicultural composition of the South African community than their predecessors. These authors' portrayal of the transcultural theme is marked by a strong tendency towards stereotyping. This tendency, however, seems not to be limited to this particular genre, but can also be found in other literary traditions belonging to this period. Some South African English literary works from this period, for instance, show strong tendencies towards racism and the stereotyping of people from other language groups. In 1926 an acknowledged author from this period, Sarah Gertrude Millin (as quoted by Coetzee 1987: 27), still expresses herself as follows with regard to some of her fellow South Africans: 'The Griqua type of half-caste ... is lower than the Kaffir.'

The tendency towards negative stereotyping is equally strong in Afrikaans literature of this period. Gerwel (1988: 204), for instance, objects to the dehumanised stereotyping of the Coloured as a childish and emotionally bankrupt being in Afrikaans literature. He also says the following with regard to Afrikaans literature published during the period 1875–1948:

> *Die letterkunde het persone van kleur nooit as komplekse problematiese wesens voorgestel nie, maar altyd as eenvoudige eenvormighede wat uitgese kan word ... in klinkklare beelde.*   (Gerwel 1988:204)
>
> This literature never depicted people of colour as complex and problematic beings, but always presented them as simplistic uniformities who could be portrayed in ... pure images.

This viewpoint is supported by Malan (1987: 4) when he says:

> Afrikaans literature, which produced its first important works at the beginning of this century, is often criticised for its initial stereotyping of people of different skin colour and its realistic portrayal of racism.

It seems, therefore, that the tendencies identified in this study are not peculiar to Xhosa prose fiction only, but are, in fact, inherent in most literary traditions from this period as Malan (1987:6) observes:

> it seems as though the writers of all languages and colour groups during the early era under discussion can be accused of indifference towards the racial issue, stereotyping and even racism.

The deficiencies outlined above could, in my view, be ascribed to various possible causes. They could, for instance, be ascribed to a general attitude of transcultural indifference which existed amongst the majority of South Africans in the past, in terms of which authors were not inclined to consider the depiction of characters beyond their own specific language group. On the more formal level, these deficiencies can also be attributed to the socio-political strategies and policies which were followed in the recent past. These strategies seriously limited mutual contact between South Africans on a transcultural basis and often led to the arousal of various forms of misperceptions amongst the various language groups concerning one another. Mphahlele, as quoted by Malan (1987: 15), therefore comes to the conclusion that:

> Because of our separate racial life blacks and whites do not know enough about each other fully to portray character across colour and racial lines.

The intensified attempts at normalisation of relations between the various language groups in the southern African region which are presently being undertaken will, it is hoped, encourage authors to experiment more freely on the transcultural level and thereby enhance the general literary quality of Xhosa prose fiction.

WORKS CITED

Coetzee, J.M., 'Blood, flaw, taint, degeneration: The case of Sarah Gertrude Millin' in C. Malan (ed.) *Race and Literature*. Sensal Publication, 15, Pinetown: Owen Burgess Publishers, 1987.

Gerwel, J., *Literatuur en Apartheid*, Kasselsvlei: Kampen Publishers, 1988.

Jordan, A.C., Ingqumbo Yeminyanya, (Ninth impression), Alice: Lovedale Press, 1980.

Malan, C. (ed.), *Introduction to Race and Literature*, Sensal Publication, 15, Pinetown: Owen Burgess Publishers, 1987.

Milbury-Steen, S.L., *European and African Stereotypes in Twentieth Century Fiction*, New York: New York University Press, 1980.

Millin, S.G., *The South Africans*, London: Constable, 1926.

Mphahlele E., 'The tyranny of place and aesthetics. The South African case' in C. Malan (ed.) *Race and Literature*, Sensal Publication, 15, Pinetown: Owen Burgess Publishers, 1987.

Mqhayi, S.E.K., *UMqhayi WaseNtabozuko*, Alice: Lovedale Press, 1964.

——— *Ityala lamawele* (Fourth impression), Alice: Lovedale Press, 1981.

——— *UDon Jadu*, Alice: Lovedale Press, n.d.

Nqheku, A., *Arola naheng ya Maburu*, Maseru: Mazenod, 1942.

Plomer, W., *Turbott Wolfe*, London: Hogarth Press, 1926.

Schoeman, P.J., *Mboza die Swazi en ander verhale*, Bloemfontein: Nasionale Pers, 1941.

Sinxo, G.B., *UNomsa*, Alice: Lovedale Press, 1922.

——— *Umfundisi waseMtuqwasi*, Alice: Lovedale Press, 1927.

——— *Umzali Wolahleko*, Alice: Lovedale Press, 1973.

Swanepoel, C.F., 'Echoes of commitment: Race relations in three Southern African literatures' in C. Malan (ed.) *Race and Literature*, Sensal Publication, 15, Pinetown: Owen Burgess Publishers, 1987.

Van Bruggen, J., *Booia*, Johannesburg: APB, 1931.

Venter, F.A., *Swart Pelgrim*, Johannesburg: APB, 1952.

White, L. and Couzens, T. (eds), *Literature and Society in South Africa*, Cape Town: Maskew Miller, 1984.

Zuma, J.J.M., *Nigabe Ngani?* Pietermaritzburg: Shuter and Shooter, 1965.

The Dynamic & Transformational Nature of Praising in Contemporary Zulu Society

Noleen S. Turner

This paper focuses attention on three areas of contemporary praising – in the political sphere, in the form of private individual praises and thirdly as it exists in the lyrics of contemporary Maskandi music. It traces the fluidity of this form of oral tradition which is able to change its focus in order to accommodate the changing needs of the people who are so inextricably linked with it. The forms under scrutiny here, of personal and political praise poetry, are seen as an ongoing contemporary counterpart of traditional oral poetry, reflecting not only a change in their actual content, but also in the function and context in which this oral poetry is performed.

Introduction

The term *izibongo* has many varied aspects to its nature, but the meaning that is most widely accepted in relation to these compositions in Zulu oral traditions, is that they are a form of oral poetry which outlines the feats, character, physical and personality features of the person or thing about whom or which they are composed.

There are four specific categories of *izibongo* which one encounters in Zulu oral traditions:

a) *Izibongo zamakhosi* – the praises of kings and chiefs which is the highest literary form of praising
b) *Izibongo zabantu* – the praises of ordinary people
c) *Izibongo zezilwane nezinyoni* – the praises of animals and birds
d) *Izibongo zezinto ezingaphili* – the praises of inanimate objects

The dynamic functions of Zulu praise poetry

Opland (1983: 236) in his extensive research on Xhosa Oral Poetry, makes the important point that: 'Tradition is not a lifeless thing; it alters and adapts to new social circumstances.' It is not only in the forms of praise

46

poetry that one encounters changes and transformations, but also in the functions that this type of poetry serves.

Izibongo zamakhosi (the praises of chiefs and kings)
In terms of this category of *Izibongo*, the contemporary monarchs find themselves in situations where they are praised alongside professional politicians in a new and dynamic form of praise poetry. Gunner and Gwala (1991: 7) make the point that 'praise poetry is a genre that has been and still is extremely open to appropriation by those who had or wished to have access to political power and influence.'

In times gone by, this form of *izibongo* was performed by an *imbongi* – a professional bard, whose function was not only to praise the king, but also to criticise him where necessary, without fear of retribution. As inter-mediary and the channel between the king and his people, the *imbongi* can be seen to have filled the function of political advisor or councillor. Gunner and Gwala (1991 :12) make the point about *izibongo* that they are available and are used in these political times, both

> within an 'authoritarian populism' and an emergent 'popular democratic' culture. They are thus at the centre of contested terrain and are a key art form in the political discourse of the day, perhaps particularly in contemporary Natal but also nationally.

Today the picture is extremely different for the modern *imbongi* compared to his traditional counterpart from days gone by. If one examines the praises of the current Zulu King as recorded by his previous *inyosi* (bard), Dlamini, one becomes aware of the fact that unlike the balanced praises of previous powerful Zulu kings from Shaka to Cetshwayo, where licence to criticise the monarch was not uncommon, these modern praises no longer contain lines which could be considered damaging or critical of the king's actions, indicating a shift in the function of the *imbongi*. With the political situation in 1996, and the tension between Inkatha and the ANC, there is little wonder that

> Usage ... of key symbolic forms [such as the royal izibongo] conveys a kind of ownership, a right to dictate and define what a culture is, to whom it belongs and how it operates in relation to contending political ideologies of the time.
> (Gunner and Gwala 1991 :12)

The political situation in Natal in 1996 resulted in an unprecedented situation where Dlamini, the former *imbongi* of the reigning Zulu monarch, King Zwelithini, refused to perform as the king's official bard because of the king's ANC political leanings. He restricted himself to praising the leader of the Inkatha Freedom Party. Politics for the first time influenced the role of the official royal *imbongi*.

In the run up to the 1996 KwaZulu Natal local elections, performances of the *imbongi* took place on occasions in rural areas where the Inkatha Freedom Party candidates were addressing their rural constituencies.

This would indicate that even the usage of praises of senior political leaders, aside from those of the royal house, has a role to play on the contemporary political scene in uniting people in support of a particular political party or ideology. Kromberg in his research clearly shows that this trend is not unique to the Inkatha Freedom Party, but was also harnessed by the ANC aligned trade unions in the late 1980s and early 1990s.

Kaschula (1991), in research conducted amongst the Xhosa, cites the cases of several *iimbongi* who have been either harassed or arrested in recent years because of criticism which has been passed about certain political leaders and contentious political issues while reciting oral praises. Vail and White (1991: 54) demonstrated the changing nature of praise poetry amongst the Ndebele from the time of Mzilikazi, to Lobengula through to the times of colonial rule, where the praise poetry changed from legitimising the ruling group, to concentrating on the virtues of national unity under the king, then to asserting 'in nostalgic and exclusive terms an injured pride in an Ndebele ethnic purity' (1991: 55). Groenewald (1996: 73) also illustrates the contemporary dynamism of praise poety amongst the Ndebele. He discusses the use of Ndebele praise poetry as a powerful contemporary political tool which is used to 'sensitise' the listeners as to the 'legitimacy' of the subject. He cites the case of Prince James Senzangakhona Mahlangu, who was a politician in the late 1980s, aspiring to a position in the now defunct KwaNdebele cabinet, whose praise poetry was used as a political weapon in the crucial year of 1988. Between July and December of 1988, in view of the proposed independence of KwaNdebele, at the seven meetings at which Groenewald recorded the material for his research, no fewer than 88 praise poems were performed. He concludes that the praise poetry of the modern political leaders such as that of James Mahlangu, has evolved from the traditional and ethnic form of poetry, and is now considered an important political tool which can be used alongside political speeches not only to reinforce but also to influence the views of the people. One has only to review the reaction of the audience to the praises of President Nelson Mandela recited at the inauguration ceremony in 1995, to realise the potential power of this form of oral poetry.

Kaschula (1991: 225) goes on to make the point that the modern *imbongi* no longer exclusively praises the local chief but is drawn towards other organisations which enjoy the support of the masses, such as political organisations, e.g. the ANC or Inkatha, as well as trade unions, which wield considerable clout on the contemporary political stage. Although the styles and techniques that are used to praise these impersonal organisations are based on the same pattern as that of *izibongo zamakhosi*, the oral tradition, because of its fluidity, is able to change its focus and accommodate the changing needs of the people who are so inextricably linked with it.

Izibongo zezinto ezingaphili (praise poetry of the inanimate)
This particular form of *izibongo* thrived in the stressful political climate of the 1980s and early 1990s in the form of praises of political parties and trade union movements. Kromberg (1994: 61) explains this phenomenon as resulting from the audience's intimacy with this form of popular oral poetry. Poetry dedicated to trade unions and political parties has been documented in *Black Mamba Rising*. Kromberg, in his research on worker *izibongo*, cites the fact that many worker poets acknowledge that they consciously draw on *izibongo* which represent a tradition with which they and the audience are familiar and with which they feel an affinity. As one of these poets who uses this approach to worker poetry which Kromberg (1994: 67) quotes so succintly expresses himself:

> We ... join the past to the present and to the future. Our poetry in the traditional form was done in the *imbongi* style. And once the person stood there and paced the stage, raised his voice, lowered his voice, screeched, pounded the air, immediately people recognised it - hey, this is poetry, let us listen!

The repetitive style used by Mzwakhe Mbuli in his brand of poetry is also steeped in the style of *izibongo*, as in this illustration:

> *Ukulimala kwengqondo, ukulimala komuntu*
> *Ukulimala komuntu, ukulimala komndeni*
> *Ukulimala komndeni kusho ukulimala kwesizwe*
>
> Injury of the mind is injury to a person
> Injury to a person is injury to the family
> Injury to the family is an injury to the nation

The popularity of the form of *izibongo* in this contemporary poetry dedicated to political parties and trade union movements is not, as Kromberg notes, something that has been instituted from above. Based on his research where enthusiastic reception has been given to this form of poetry amongst the workers, he argues that the demand has been from below and reflects an ongoing partiality for such forms among the broad membership of labour and political organisations. The poets which Kromberg cites clearly identify their use of *izibongo* as a 'weapon' to advance their political beliefs. Apart from the praises of inanimate political bodies such as trade unions, the praises of inanimate things is something which still occurs, often with a shift of emphasis in modern urban settings. It is not uncommon to encounter taxi drivers praising their vehicles, or people praising their cars in the same way that their rural counterparts may praise their livestock.

Izihasho zabantu

In this day and age on the contemporary social scene, personal praising has also proved itself to be a dynamic and relevant form of oral communication and expression. *Izibongo zabantu* are poems composed in contemporary times about ordinary people and are often referred to as *izihasho*. Koopman has touched on the subject of the praises of young Zulu men as an extension of his research on Zulu personal names, and he cites examples of typical courting, dancing and fighting, as well as some boxing and football praise names. Psychologically, in Zulu society a person is the cluster of his names, which are the core of his *izibongo*. They record him 'warts and all', and do not aspire to the level of the elevated eulogies that befit the person of rank, importance or royalty. This does not, however, rob them of their 'spice' – on the contrary, it enhances them, as in this type of poetry there is nothing at stake (except the target's reputation). The ordinary man's praises are but an extension of his 'being'. In this form of oral poetry where praising is predominant, a person may also be criticised in a satirical light using the traditionally recognised framework or form of *izibongo*. The style of composition of *izibongo* and *izihasho* is the same as far as form and poetic techniques used, and differs only in content. These *izihasho* can be seen as an ongoing contemporary counterpart of traditional oral poetry, and it is in this particular form that we encounter panegyric and satire being complementary forms of amplification.

The praises of men

The link of a man's personality and identity is so tied in with his praises that they are not confined to the traditional performing situations of dance, song and 'praises', i.e. *ukugiya*. These praises are of an informal nature, are composed by non-professional composers, and are normally recited at non-formal occasions, e.g. when men sit together under a tree to talk, drink and swop ideas, where any new arrival to the circle of men sitting down sharing a pot of beer will be greeted by his praises, or he may even recite them himself. In more recent times, praises can be heard being called out on the playing fields – before, during or after a soccer or boxing match – by a man's supporters as in the example cited below. They may, however, be recited as a form of encouragement in whatever field of endeavour an individual may be engaged in, sportwise or not.

'Izibongo zikaMhlambi' (Soccer Praises)

Umchachambi wegazi
Umbambo kazibalwa
Kazibalwa ikhulu lamadoda
Esistadium kwaMashu

Umkitazi wezintombi
Kuhlek' onina
Udovadova isikhumba
Senj' endala

The hot blooded one!
The ribs cannot be counted
Counted by so many
At KwaMashu stadium

The joker-with-girls
The mothers are pleased to see him.
Continuous kicker of the ball.

The first line refers to this man as a hot blooded Casanova. The first and second lines refer to a bad fall he had during a soccer match where he broke many ribs at the soccer stadium in KwaMashu. The third and fourth lines refer to his popularity not only with the ladies, but also with prospective mothers-in-law! The last two lines encapsulate the lovely de-ideophonic metaphor of continuous pounding describing the man as a soccer player who is able to relentlessly kick the ball, which is described literally as the skin of an old dog – signifying the smoothness of the soccer ball which has no hair, just like an old dog.

'Dancing Praises'

Qephuza Mgabadeli!
Mthunzi wokuphumula amatshitshi namajongosi,
S'buko samaqhikiza.
Ishaye mfo kaQhothwane!
Kukikize izinkehli zikhala,
Zithi mfana wazalelwani muva,
Ngoba nathi ngabe sithola umthunzi wokukhosela.

Dance Mgabadeli!
Shade of resting virgins and young girls,
Mirror of senior girls.
Do it, son of Qhothwane!
The old ladies voice their appreciation crying,
Saying, 'young man, why were you born so late,
Because we would get shelter under your shade.'

These praises exhort this young man to greater heights in his dancing performance. Line 2 is a typical formula which is often used to refer to an *isoka* or man who is popular with women. The last two lines are a humorous interjection implying that even the older women bemoan the fact that this virile young dancer was born too late for them to have a chance at romancing him.

'Courting Praises'

Thang' elimil' endlini
Amany' emil' ezaleni
Izintombi zimcel' ukhisi
Noma ejahile.

Izintombi ziyamgagamela
Abanye behla benyuka
Beya emfuleni

Zith' ezinye izinsizwa zisabalele nemifula
Wena ube uzicwalela ibheshu lakho.

Pumpkin which grows in the house
Whilst others grow on the dumping site.
You whom girls ask for a kiss
Even if you are in a hurry.

You whom girls approach
Whilst others go up and down to the river
While other fellows are scattered at the rivers
You are busy beautifying your gear.

These lines are dedicated to a handsome fellow who was very popular with females in his area. The first line indicates his uniqueness, just as pumpkin seeds commonly grow around dumping sites, this unlikely one has grown inside the house – something that is quite unusual. The following lines also indicate his incredible popularity with the girls.

The first line in the second stanza refers to the unusual occurrence where girls make the first approach to this Casanova, not the usual custom amongst the Zulus. The last three lines refer to the fact that he does not have to bother with searching for 'talent' at the river banks where young girls would go to draw water, like the other young men would do, he just needs to relax at home preparing himself for his next courting exploit.

Where criticism does occur in *izibongo* it may be seen as an attempt to exert a form of social control on a purely inter-personal, community level. As well as exposing a person's weakness and failings, the uncomplimentary references may also serve the purpose of creating an ironical self esteem in the person whereby his praises are a means of making him or her accept any physical or behavioural oddity he/she may have, without developing any inferiority complex about these perceived failings.

One such character is derided in the example below for his shortcomings in being an outrageous womaniser insofar as he targets very young girls and married women:

'Izibongo zikaS'guiana'

Wadlala magumbela kwesakhe
Bathi Umondli wezintandane
Bhojabhoja nkunzi engeninazo izithola
Ngisho nalezo esezisale emizileni
Magiya ngezihlangu zamanye amadoda
Ingabe uyosisika nini esakho?

Mazond' amatshitshi nezinkehli
Maphephela kwezisanuka ubisi
Lapho umashayndawonye esegasele
Uzibe ngokuthi zibanjwa zisemaphuphu
Maqhamuka emaqeleni maqedane
Lezo ezisafufusa zithi nyawo zami ngibelethe!

Klebe ohamba phansi ingathi
Abanye bandizela phezulu.
Usibaya sibuswa yinkabi
Kanti ezinye zibuswa zinkunzi.
Nkunzi emdwayidwa ngenxa yameva
Kanti ezinye zimdwayidwa ngenxa yokuba zibovulana.

You play you selfish one
They say you are the provider of orphans
Pierce oh bull that doesn't have any calves.
Even those who are left on the paths (unchosen ones)
One who dances using other men's shields
When will you cut your own?

The hater of young and mature girls
The one who prefers those who are still immature
When you strike in one place and still continue attacking
You pretend by saying that they are caught while still young.
The one who when he appears in the veld
Those who are still young run away

The hawk that hovers low down
While others fly at great height above
Kraal that is governed by an ox
Whilst others are governed by bulls.
Bull which is scratched by thorns
Whilst others are scratched from fighting one another.

This extremely rich and allusive poem denigrates this man who has no legal children of his own, but 'takes care' of those in need/unprovided for, referring to his irresponsible sexual exploits (lines 1–4) as he has no wife/girlfriend of his own. Lines 5 and 6 refer to his tendency to have affairs with other men's wives. The second verse refers to his preference for sex with very young girls, whilst the third verse sarcastically refers to his impotency (the comparison of *inkabi* to *inkunzi* – bull to ox) and calls attention in the last two lines to his cowardly behaviour.

The praises of women

Despite the predominance of *izibongo* in the male domain, recent research shows increasing proliferation of this oral poetry amongst females, not only in rural but also in urban areas. Gunner, who has done extensive research on the *izibongo* of women in rural areas, cites the function of *izibongo* as 'a poetic statement of identity' (1979: 241). A woman's acquaintances will acknowledge her indirectly or greet her directly by referring to one or more lines of her praise names. She goes on to say that 'the women who possess and compose praise poems are usually traditionalists who do not belong to any of the mission churches, and many are married in polygynous households' (1979: 239). Apart from the function of 'poetic identity' which Gunner cites, she also lists complaint and accusation as important functions of these praise poems. Tension and rivalries that exist in the close knit structure of the Zulu polygamous unit find their legitimate outlet in praise poetry through allusive diction. Gunner states that 'The statement of complaint or accusation in a praise poem is an effective and socially acceptable way of publicly announcing one's anger or grief' (1979: 239). Finnegan (1970: 470) reinforces this point when she states that:

> Names often play an indispensable part in oral literature in Africa ... they have ... many different interpretations ... from the psychological functions of names, in providing assurance or 'working out' tension, to their connection with the structure of society, their social function in minimizing friction, or their useful-ness either in expressing the self-image of their owner *or in providing a means of indirect comment when a direct one is not feasible.*

This is clearly evident in the following praises of MaGumbi which are recited in an attempt to level criticism at the co-wife in a polygamous marriage situation:

'Izibongo zikaMaGumbi'

Wema Sonjinji,
Ngilala njengawe.
Woza uzongibona.

You, the daughter of Sonjinji ,
I sleep just like you do.
Come and see me.

Here the accusation is levelled by the first wife at the second who boasts about the fact that the husband prefers to sleep with her. These lines are recited by MaGumbi in the presence of other women to let her counterpart know that the husband also sleeps just as contentedly with her, and she invites her to verify the fact. The name Sonjinji is a fictitious one as this deflects direct accusation. The co-wife, however, as well as MaGumbi supporters are well aware who the target of the reference is.

Women who live in rural areas have a far more prolific collection of praises than their urban counterparts. The reason for this is to be found in the very nature of their communal existence. By reciting or having one's praises recited, one's sense of belonging within a particular community or cultural group is reinforced. As women's praises are normally performed in the presence of other women – within the homestead, in the fields while working or at any social occasion – 'the feeling of group solidarity and a shared identity is often very strong' (Gunner 1979: 243). Praises can be self-composed or given by one's peers. They may comprise lines that arise from both these sources. The performance of these praises is a communal experience and as such the balance between praise and dispraise or com-plaint motif encountered in the majority of the oral poetry of rural women, is more marked. Although there may well be uncomplimentary references and accusations against others, these are often balanced with those that serve to compliment and flatter the subject as in the following example:

'Izibongo zikaManzoyi waKwaNdelu' (S. Mnguni)

Umagawul' egijima
Ugqinsi lakwaNdelu
Olwagqinsil' abafazi
Babuya bengayitholanga

Undoda phumel' eshashalazini
Ngikugob' inkani
Undod' iyangabazu
Abafazi bathithibele

The one who chops and runs
The heavy faller of the Ndelu people
She who comes down heavily on the women
They return without receiving it.

Man come to the stage
I yield to your stubbornness
The man is hesitant
The women are at a loss at what to do.

These complimentary praises of this well known figure in her area
describe primarily her nature and her dancing prowess. Line 1 refers to
the speed with which she performs, whereas the ideophone in line 2
describes her physically as heavy. This image is carried on into the third
line where there is an ideophonic reflection of her solid heavy dancing
style. Line 4 reflects her superiority to others when dancing the *ingoma*
style of dance, the allusive reference deriving from the fact that when
women are dancing and the audience do not think they are quite up to
scratch, they are wont to say out loud 'Buya uma ungayithola' (return
when you get it– that is, become successful at performing *ingoma* dance).
MaNzoyi is well known in her community for her fighting ability which
surfaced when she was still a child and was victorious in fights against
young boys. This fearlessness transcends into her dancing ability and she
is known to challenge men in their dancing skills. Line 6 is the attitude
that most people in the area have towards her, hence this saying used
about her. The final two lines of the poem summarise her ability by saying
that not only are the men hesitant to challenge her, but she completely
overawes the women.

In addition to *izibongo* serving to praise a woman for her praiseworthy
qualities, they may also expose her indiscretions or bad behaviour as in
the following two examples.

'Izibongo zikaMaNgcobo'

Ubuqili bentethe,
Sengathi ibelethe ingane
Kanti ibelethe indoda.

Cunning of the locust,
Which looks as if it is carrying a child on its back
Whereas it carries a man.

In these humorous praises of MaNgcobo reference is made to an incident where she was having an extra-marital affair with a man within the confines of her in-laws' homestead, while her husband was doing contract labour at the mines. This crafty lady overcame the problem of being discreet by putting her short lover on her back and covering him with a blanket as if she was carrying a child.

The oral poetry encountered in contemporary urban settings (see Turner 1995) which reflects a lifestyle which is not as close knit as that of women in rural environments, nevertheless reveals that all members of urban society hold a basic shared value-system and therefore feel at liberty to comment through the lines recited in the oral poems of their peers, on any form of behaviour that affects the stability and smooth running of their societal setting. The following oral poem chastises a woman for her loose behaviour in the location of Lindela in Eshowe:

'Izibongo zikaMaZuma eLindelani'

Ugxamalaza mfazi
Kuvela amapitikoti.
Usifebe asikhathali
Uhulala emajoyintini.

Woman who sits in a bad fashion
Exposing the petticoat.
You are a prostitute who does not tire
Ever present in the shebeens.

The highly critical nature of these praises reveals the shortcomings of this woman who is known to frequent shebeens in her location. These lines are composed and recited by her fellow women. The censure contained therein is, however, accepted by her and when these lines are recited, normally when she gets up to *gida*, they serve to egg her on and the censure does not cause any ill-feeling whatsoever.

Okpewho, in his research on African oral literature (1993), explains that speaking about one's problems, whether in the form of song, poetry or story, provides the performer with an avenue for emotional and psychological release in day-to-day relations between members of society, helping to promote the bases for social harmony. He notes that this form of oral lampooning is widespread across Africa. The type of oral poetry encountered in the praises of women from both rural and urban environments, accounts for its ongoing contemporary popularity as it is used as an acceptable means of social commentary and deflection of ill-feeling that may occur in situations where women live in close proximity.

Praises in Maskandi music

Another modern form of popular praising is that which occurs in Maskandi music. This is a type of neo-traditional instrumental music popular amongst the Zulu people which is played on Western instruments such as the guitar, concertina, violin, piano accordion, electric guitars and drums. The word is derived from the Afrikaans word 'musikant'. This form of music developed its popularity in the early part of the twentieth century when migrant labour became commonplace in South Africa. Men would leave their homes in rural areas to find work in mines or in towns in various industries and would play their instruments and sing for the purpose of entertaining themselves (or others), as well as relieving boredom, depression and homesick feelings. The lyrics of certain songs may be sung with the specific purpose of winning over a girl, or to express some lovesick emotions, as a commentary on a particular social condition or occurrence, or even to chastise, denigrate or censure some particular person's behaviour.

Critical lyrics often contain a social message for the audience or may even carry a political message as most Maskandi musicians believe they have an important role to play in society by reflecting on things both positive and negative in the community around them. Most often the lyrics of the song are appreciated because the theme reflects 'traditional' Zulu values and beliefs. In contrast to rural artists, many urban performers either sustain themselves solely on their art, or they have other jobs which provide them with income, their performances being part-time. However, as the modern city environment is a melting pot of people from various communities and ethnic groups, the urban artist is known to far fewer people on a personal basis and his audience often does not relate to him outside the arena of performance, unlike his counterpart in the villages and country areas where the artist and his fellow citizens were known to one another.

It is for this reason primarily, that we encounter the phenomenon of praising embedded within the lyrics of Maskandi music, where the artist, apart from fulfilling the role of entertainer, is able to manipulate the material he is delivering in a way that is typical of the oral tradition in performance. The audience is also far more likely to be impressed by the performer who shows some resourcefulness with the text of his song, than by one who sticks to a set pattern and delivers his lines mechanically. These songs share many poetic features that are found in ordinary *izibongo*, as well as the customary introductory 'formulas' that are used by the majority of singers, which introduce the song in a certain acceptable way with which the audience is familiar. Ntuli (1990: 304) points out that the introductory formulas are addressed to the second person as with:

'*Zibambe mfo kasibanibani*' (take hold of it, brother of so and so)

'*Khuluma nazo*' (Speak to them)
'*Awuzwe-ke*' (Just listen)

The first few lines seem to indicate that the poet is addressing someone else, then he moves the focus subtly from the second person to himself as we are given his name, his praise names, his surname and the name of his father, as well as details of his origins. According to Nollene Davies who has done extensive research on Maskandi music:

> Izibongo are important because that is what makes people happy. It tells about that particular person, his life and so on. It is indispensable when singing to people. They must know things about you, your life, hardships, stories, etc.

She goes on to say

> The praises provide the musician with a source of inspiration and he becomes 'spirited' ... the praises contain humour and satire and reflect many of the features found in other Zulu *izibongo*: highly developed poetic language, frequent use of metaphors, imagery, repetitions and other features. A musician may also include criticism of people which would not be permissable outside the context of the song.   (Davies, 1992:63).

Praises are not fixed within the lyrics of songs. The musician may recite lines of his *izibongo* at will while playing various songs, or he may choose to omit them altogether. This is evidence of the oral links this music form has, and the mercurial nature of praises, which rely very much on the frame of mind of the praiser, the context within which he is praising, and the reaction of the people before whom he is performing. The praises are not sung, but are recited at high speed in the way that an *imbongi* would normally recite praises. The content of the praises tends to focus on the singer's origins, the place where he was born with mention of the local mountain and river, the name of his forebears, and some lines of personal praise. The example of praising within the lyrics of a song given in the Appendix, is one which was recorded by Davies of a talented Maskandi musician, Shiyani Ngcobo, in which he expresses his concern with the Shembite religion and the difficulty he has as a Zulu person with a traditional upbringing, in accepting it as a relevant religion for the Zulu people. He accuses the Shembites of being discriminatory in that they propagate Shembe as their religious icon, rejecting the figure of Jesus Christ as a god for foreigners.

His praises (in section 7 of the Appendix) outline his genealogy and his background and then go on to complain about the severe criticism he came in for from his community for an affair he engineered with a woman with the help of a love potion from his local *inyanga*. He then praises himself as a successful lover. Maskandi praises often include a few lines which may have something to do with the actual theme of the song before getting on to the actual lines of self praise, these lines being recited in the same manner as the actual praises, as with the lines which are recorded in section 6 of the Appendix.

Ntuli (1990: 305) succinctly evaluates the essence of praise poetry in Maskandi music when he says

> The end product is a unique type of traditional art with a multidimensional appeal to the recipient: an impressive melody, significant lyrics and rich poetry all put together.

Conclusion

Gunner and Gwala (1991: 13) comment on the ongoing appeal and adaptability of the elevated Royal Zulu praises in the following way:

> Certainly the slippery, resilient nature of the great praises has given them a capacity to be constantly interpreted anew; they exist at different times in different relations to the historical moment and this has meant that even the royal praises, including even those of Shaka, have not been captured and contained within a narrow, exclusively ethnic ideology.

In the political sphere, praising has been adapted to accommodate the needs of the people who use it and is a clear illustration of how this form of oral poetry is transformational not so much in form, but in the function it fulfils.

In examining the nature of *izibongo/izihasho zabantu*, important points to take into consideration when analysing these contemporary and dynamic oral texts, are context and function. The performance is not complete in itself - it exists within a recognised tradition. The impact that the recitation of these various forms of praises has, not only on the person at whom they are directed, but also on the people present, is totally reliant on the environment in which they are recited and also on who is responsible for reciting them. This will often also determine the function intended in the articulation of a person's praises.

Generally, the lines of 'praises' are known by people close to the recipient in their community. In some of these examples, the oral poem seems to be used as a form of reprimand but the severity of the chastisement depends largely on the context, and may vary from mild and playful teasing, to deprecation or derogation. The *izibongo* may be used to directly censure a person about their behaviour, or they may be used indirectly to target someone else in the community, whose actions are deemed unacceptable.

Where the content of an oral poem contains criticism and not exclusively praise, it often does not provoke hostility or animosity by means of the humour embedded in the images and the context in which it is recited. Where humour is lacking in the actual words, it may be very much part of the performance with the reciter softening the message by absurd facial expressions and bodily gestures to motivate laughter. This ultimately will reveal whether the person is being chastised or not, or whether the articulation of a person's praises is meant to delight and excite the recipient. This results from the fact that attention and acknowledgement of one's character are being focused on him/her. Among one's peers, the recitation of a person's praises elevates him/her and is not necessarily taken as an admonishment or insult, despite the seemingly censorious or insulting overtones in the poem. Being known by one's 'praises' provides the person with a distinct identity, a sort of recognition and support which is important to his/her ego and psyche and for this very reason, they remain a popular and often necessary form of public expression in the acceptable form of poetry.

Okpewho endorses this viewpoint in his research on the impact of praising in African communities, where he makes the point that praising can be seen as a means of

> discouraging social evils such as theft, adultery, truancy and general irresponsibility among young and old alike. ... they encourage the citizens of a society, to observe proper conduct, cultivate a sense of purpose and responsibility, and issue a warning whenever anyone or any group indulges in habits that are detrimental to the moral health and general survival of the society. (1993: 149)

Far from being a dying art form, 'praising' in contemporary Zulu society continues to flourish, to adapt and to gain momentum in its modern and dynamic setting. Where transformation in content and even presentation may occur, *izibongo* continue to reflect the origins of this traditional oral poetic form which has flourished amongst the Zulu people since time immemorial.

Appendix

Ukholo lwakwashembe - the shembite religion

1. *Wo! Khuzani kuyonakala*
    Be wary of this – things are getting out of hand!
    Ukholo IwakwaShembe alulungile,
    Shembe's religion is not good
    Alulunganga nje.
    Its not good.
    Wo! Khuzani kuyonakala,
    Ukholo IwakwaShembe alulungile
    Luyabandlulula madoda,
    It discriminates, men,
    Ngoba luthi uJesu uyinkosi yaphesheya.
    Because it says Jesus is Lord from overseas
    Thina mabhinca sikholwe kanjani na?
    What should we heathens believe?
    Uma nithi uJesu uyinkosi yaphesheya?
    When you say Jesus is the Lord from overseas?

Thina mabhinca sikholwe kanjani no?
What must we heathens believe?

2. *Wo! Khuzani kuyonakala,*
   Ukholo IwakwaShembe alulungile luyabandlulula,
   Wo! Khuzani kuyonakala, ukholo IwakwaShembe, maZulu
      luyabandlulula.
   Wo! Khuzani kuyonakala,
   Ukholo IwakwaShembe, maZulu luyabandlulula nje,
   Ngoba luthi uJesu uyinkosi yaphesheya.
   Thina mabhinca sikholwe kanjani na?
   Abantu sebexabene ezitimeleni oh.
   People are quarrelling on the trains.

3. *Ukholo IwakwaShembe alulungile, alulunganga,*
   Luxabanisa abantu
   It makes people fight
   Ukholo IwakwaShembe alulungile alulungangu,
   Luxabanisa abantu.

4. Repeat of verses 1 & 2

5. Repeat of verse 3

6. (INTRODUCTION TO PRAISES)
   Khuluma nazo, Shiyani bathakathi!
   Speak to them, forget/leave the sorcerers!
   Nabulala naqeda umsebenzi, madoda.
   You are killing and destroying your work, men.
   Ngosuku olulodwa, uyosebenzani kusasa
   In one day, where will you find it tomorrow
   Badiliziwe abantu bagcwele imigwaqo,
   Retrenched people are crowding the streets,
   Emsebenzini nakhu bayawuphanga
   Because they hurriedly finish their work
   Umsebenzi, madoda musani ukuwuphanga
   Don't rush the work men,
   Umsebenzi ngosuku olulodwa nje.
   Don't destroy the work in one day.

(ACTUAL PRAISES)
Kwasho uSiklebhe indoda, engizalayo kanjalo,
So said Siklebhe, my father
Ubaba lo engikhuluma ngaye, madoda
I'm talking about my father, men
Khona eMthwalume la ngibuye khona,
From Mthwalume where I come from
Umfula engiwuphuzayo phezulu enhla nawo.
I drink from this river's fountain
Wakhuluma nazo ngempela umthakathi wentombi
Talk to them, one who has bewitched a girl
Engayithumela ngezizwe
Because I bewitched the maiden with hysteria with muthi
Engazinikwa abasenyangeni ngangayizeka
Which I was given by the inyangas, but I did not marry her

Bangihlawulisa ngibathengile.
They punished me although I paid them
Indumandumane phela edume ngothando emantombazaneni.
The one who is famous because of his love exploits amongst the
    young maidens.
Nithini madoda? Nizwa kanjani makukhulunywa kanjalo manje?
What do you say men about this?
Musani ukusibandlulula nina madoda!
Don't discriminate against us, you men!

WORKS CITED

Davies, N.J., *A Study of the Guitar Styles in Zulu Maskanda Music.* Unpublished MA Thesis, University of Natal, Durban, 1992.
Finnegan, R., *Oral Literature in Africa*, Oxford: Clarendon Press, 1970.
Gunner, E., 'Songs of Innocence and Experience: Zulu Women as Composers and Performers of izibongo, Zulu Praise Poems', *Research in African Literatures* 10. 2: 228–56, 1979.
—— 'Ukubonga nezibongo: Zulu Praising and Praises'. Unpublished PhD thesis, University of London, 1984.
Gunner, E. and Gwala, M., *Musho! Zulu Popular Praises*, Johannesburg: Witwatersrand University Press, 1991.
Groenewald, H.M., 'In Praise of Resistance.' Unpublished paper presented at SAFOS Conference Pilansberg, 1994.
Kaschula, R. H., 'The Transitional Role of the Xhosa Oral Poet in Contemporary South African Society'. Unpublished PhD thesis, Grahamstown: Rhodes University, 1991.
Kromberg, S., 'Worker Izibongo and Ethnic Identities in Durban', *Journal of Literary Studies* 10. 1: 57–74, 1994.
Ntuli, D.B.Z., 'Remarks on Maskandi Poetry', *S A Journal of African Languages* 10. 4: 302–6, 1990.
Okpewho, I., *African Oral Literature*, Bloomington: Indiana University Press, 1993.
Opland, J., *Xhosa Oral Poetry*, Cambridge: Cambridge University Press, 1983.
Sitas, Ari (ed.), *Black Mamba Rising*, Durban: Culture and Working Life Project, 1989.
Turner, N.S., 'Censure and Social Comment in the *izihasho* of Urban Zulu Women', *Alternation* 2. 2: 55–73, 1995.
Vail, L. and White, L., *Power and the Praise Poem*, Charlottesville: University Press of Virginia, 1991.

'Structures of Feeling' & Constructions of History
Mazisi Kunene's
Emperor Shaka the Great

Duncan Brown

In 1993 Mazisi Kunene was declared Poet Laureate of Africa by UNESCO in a ceremony in Morocco. This declaration was greeted with both jubilation and bewilderment in South Africa. Those who approved suggested that it reflected a long-overdue honouring of a poet insufficiently recognised in his own country and continent; while others asked – mostly covertly – why Kunene should be so honoured, who felt that Africa needed a Poet Laureate, what the concept of 'Africa' implied by the title actually meant, and on what basis UNESCO felt it had the jurisdiction to make such an award? And yet Kunene's being honoured as an 'African' poet by this organisation representing the 'international' community is in many ways appropriate in terms of the concerns of his work and the trajectory of his life; and the combination of jubilation and covert questioning which greeted the award reflects something of the anomalous position and reception of this poet both in his own country and abroad. In this article I wish to engage seriously with Mazisi Kunene and his place in literary history, through an analysis of what is arguably his best-known work, *Emperor Shaka the Great* (1979). I shall suggest the real possibilities and strengths of this poem, while acknowledging the often contradictory 'structures of feeling' that inform and impel it.

Large critical claims have been made for Kunene's work by, amongst others, Albert S. Gérard who talks of Kunene's 'considerable talent and striking originality in [his] use of traditional Zulu concepts and imagery' (1981: 217), and Kodiatu Sesay who claims that Kunene is 'certainly one of the best black writers in [South Africa] today' (1988: 61). Referring specifically to *Emperor Shaka the Great* Ken Goodwin says, 'This is, I believe, a great epic or at least one verging on greatness' (1982:188), and Ursula A. Barnett concurs that 'it may possibly stand beside some of the world's great epics' (1983: 108). While there are frequent references in passing to Kunene in critical studies of African and South African literature, however, few critics have engaged the poetry in any sustained or serious manner, or in many cases *even read* it. Those critical discussions which do exist have tended to be simply valorising (with the exception of those by John Haynes (1987), Mbongeni Z Malaba (1988), and Ari Sitas (1994)). I wish in this article to give substance to the approbative claims for his work while at the same time cutting through the mythologising of the poet and his work which obscures some of its very real difficulties.

My reasons for focusing on *Emperor Shaka the Great* are various, not least because I think it is one of Kunene's finest achievements. However, the poem is particularly fascinating in taking as its subject one of the most important, and contested, historical figures in South African history.[1] In KwaZulu Natal, Shaka has been appropriated by various political and commercial interest groups, and the 'story of Shaka' is in many ways the lived text of the region's past and present. As well as being taken up as a justificatory symbol or myth for much political mobilisation and conflict, it informs almost every other aspect of life – from religious devotion in churches such as *ibandla lamaNazaretha* (the Church of the Nazarites) and others, to debates about the location of the provincial capital and the role of traditional leaders in a modern democratic state. The image of Shaka has even recently been appropriated by the KwaZulu Natal Tourism Board, which has promoted a recreated and Disneyfied 'Shakaland', has mooted plans to build a seven-storey statue of Shaka at the entrance to Durban harbour, and is considering employing a praise poet to mime the praises of Shaka for ships entering the port!

Kunene was born in Durban, South Africa, in 1930. His father was from the royal Swazi clan and his mother from the large Zulu Ngcobo family. He was educated at the University of Natal, where he completed a seminal MA study on Zulu literature (the thesis was later incorporated into the Introduction to his collection *Zulu Poems*). He left South Africa in 1959 when he won a scholarship to study at the School of Oriental and African Studies (SOAS), University of London. He was already politically active in the ANC, and despite his own reluctance to take up the scholarship, he was encouraged by the organisation to use the opportunity to help get the boycott movement going (Wilkinson 1992: 140). He became the official United Nations representative of the ANC, and later its director of finance. He travelled to Europe and the United States where he gave a number of lectures. He worked at Stanford, and was later appointed Professor of African Literature and Language at UCLA. On 1 April 1966, he was banned by a *Government Gazette Extraordinary* under the Amendment to the Suppression of Communism Act (along with a number of other black South African writers). After 30 years in exile, he returned to South Africa and in 1993 took up a professorship in Zulu Language and Literature at the University of Natal, from which he is now retired. He published a number of poems either in Zulu or in translation, as well as several articles on Zulu philosophy and cosmology. His books include *Zulu Poems* (1970), *Emperor Shaka the Great* (1979), *Anthem of the Decades* (1981) and *The Ancestors and the Sacred Mountain* (1982).

Kunene's formative influences as writer and academic are very much those of Africanist debates within the ANC prior to his leaving the country, the politics of exile, and the agendas of African studies intellectuals in the US. Indeed, Kunene's reputation remains high amongst many African studies scholars abroad. One of the difficulties in conducting a study of this nature from South Africa involves actually finding what has been said about him in overseas journals. Though the lack of detailed critical attention to his work may proceed in part from what David Dorsey (1988) identifies as a broader inability/reluctance in literary studies to engage in detailed poetic analysis of African poems, Kunene's own historical position is clearly also significant in this regard. He was himself in exile, and his books were banned for distribution (though not possession) in South Africa, and were hence not freely available inside the country. Further, the tendency of literary commentaries on Kunene both in South Africa and abroad to be largely uncritical is entirely understandable considering Kunene's own banning and the context of the broader anti-apartheid struggle which required united opposition. However, more complex engagements are not only possible now, but, I would argue, necessary if we are to evaluate fully the contribution and implications of his work; and if we are, more broadly, to engage with any success in processes of social reconstruction and national (re)definition, including contributing to global understandings of local, national and international identities.

In the introduction to *Emperor Shaka the Great*, Kunene spells out what he perceives to be the purpose of his poem. He talks of cutting 'through the thick forest of propaganda and misrepresentation that [has] been submitted by colonial reports and historians ... to present an honest view of the achievements of Shaka' (1979: xiii).[2] It becomes very clear in the introduction, and in the poem itself, that Kunene's purpose is not just to exculpate the individual figure of Shaka as Zulu ruler, but to assert the importance and possibilities of the figures and institutions of African leadership more broadly. To this end, Kunene describes Shaka as 'this incredible African genius' (xxii); and he frequently elides the distinction between 'African' and 'Zulu'. This semantic equation of the terms is a specific part of Kunene's project, for he is clearly influenced by Negritude and Africanist debates. However, it sets up tensions in the poem between 'ethnic' and 'national' identifications; tensions which are partly deliberate and partly inadvertent, I think, and which are matched by the ambiguities of form – and of the 'structures of feeling' – within the poem. The ethnic/national tensions in the poem are evident particularly to readers in present-day South Africa, as the conservative organisation Inkatha has mobilised notions of Zulu cultural identity and history in the service of separatist political ends, specifically against the perceived Africanism or non-racialism of the ANC.

Before we proceed to more detailed analysis of Kunene's poem, some discussion of the concept of the 'structure of feeling' is necessary. Raymond Williams proposes this term to describe the process of dealing with texts at a remove from one's own experience, specifically those from the past:

> The most difficult thing to get hold of, in studying any past period, is this felt sense of the quality of life at a particular place and time: a sense of the ways in which the particular activities combined into a way of thinking and living. (1961: 47)

This 'felt sense' is distinct from the more formally and informally learned attitudes and perceptions which Williams refers to as 'social character' (quoting Fromm) or the 'pattern of culture' (quoting Benedict) (1961: 47). In trying to define this felt sense, he talks of

> a particular sense of life, a particular community of experience hardly needing expression, through which the characteristics of our way of life that an external analyst could describe are in some way passed, giving them a particular and characteristic colour. We are usually most aware of this when we notice the contrasts between generations, who never talk quite 'the same language', or when we read an account of our lives by someone from outside the community, or watch the small differences in style, of speech or behaviour, in someone who has learned our ways yet was not bred in them. Almost any formal description would be too crude to express this nevertheless quite distinct sense of a particular and native style. And if this is so, in a way of life we know intimately, it will surely be so when we ourselves are in the position of the visitor, the learner, the guest from a different generation: the position, in fact, that we are all in, when we study a past period . Though it can be turned to trivial account, the fact of such a characteristic is neither trivial nor marginal; it feels quite central.
>
> The term I would suggest to describe it is *structure of feeling*: it is as firm and definite as 'structure' suggests, yet it operates in the most delicate and least tangible parts of our activity. In one sense, this particular structure of feeling is the culture of a period: it is the particular living result of all the elements in the general organization. (1961: 48)

Williams stresses that the 'structure of feeling' does not presuppose a uniform social experience. He argues that it is not 'possessed in the same way by the many individuals in the community' (1961: 48); that (amongst other things) the coexistence of different generations within societies means that different structures of feeling may simultaneously be operative; and that a structure of feeling may (as in the South African context) itself involve a sense of division and social tension. While Williams's concern is specifically with the problems of literary history, his ideas seem to me to have important implications for writers' – such as Kunene's – negotiations of the disparate geographical, political and temporal contexts of writing and reception at home and in exile. Mongane Serote's comments about the brutality of exile for a writer suggest exactly this remove from the structure of feeling of one's home:

> I think there are very basic things a writer survives on: the minute-to-minute experiences of our people; the smells in this country; the sense that one

develops when one hears conversations within South Africa influenced by local events. I was denied this. So in that regard I've always said exile is a brutal assault on writers ... . (Brown 1992: 145)

Kunene appears to have been profoundly influenced by the Africanist line within the ANC in the late 1950s. Clearly this resonated with his own sense of the value of the social and cultural traditions within which he had been raised, and motivated his choice of subject-matter for his MA thesis. In exile his own sense of the importance of reasserting indigenous cultural, social and philosophical traditions was affirmed within the pan-Africanist agendas of African politics in the 1960s, and the concerns of African studies scholars in the US to recuperate notions of 'blackness' and 'Africanness'. Kunene in fact wrote an Introduction to the 1969 edition of Aimé Césaire's *Return to my Native Land* which indicated his endorsement of many of the tenets of Negritude.

Something of the way these influences swirl together into a 'structure of feeling' which permeates Kunene's project in *Emperor Shaka the Great* is suggested by his comments about indigenous literary production in apartheid South Africa. Published literature in Zulu, Xhosa and other African languages had become stultified by the system of Bantu Education and its promotion of debased versions of 'tribal' history and life, and as early as 1968 Kunene had said of this writing: 'never in our entire history has literature been so childish, so trite, so aimless' (Gérard 1981: 216). In contrast, Kunene stressed that poetry should concern itself with 'long-term national and social goals' (Haynes 1987: 53), and he defined such goals as including the creation of a 'national ego' for the broader purposes of 'nation building' (Duerden and Pieterse 1982: 89). In accordance with the tenets of Negritude, he saw the rebuilding of Zulu/African society as enlarging and restoring humanity worldwide, and his definition of 'the nation' includes, at various points, Zulu people, African people and all people, a point to which I shall return later in the article in considering critiques of his poem.

Kunene's concern with the value of indigenous traditions and especially languages is reflected in the fact that *Emperor Shaka the Great*, like all his poems, was originally written in Zulu. However, it has appeared in print only in English (and in a limited Japanese edition). Kunene admits that the translation process involved some abridgement: 'The translation of the epic does not claim to correspond word for word with the original Zulu epic. I have tried to give a faithful but free translation of the original. I have also cut out a great deal of material which would seem a digression from the story, a style unacceptable in English but characteristic of deep scholarship in Zulu' (xxvii).[3] While the decision to publish in English may be understandable in terms of market, particularly considering Kunene's position in exile and his being banned in his own country, it raises difficult questions about implied audience. In the introduction and in the direct address of the narrator to the readership in the poem, Kunene

uses first-person plural pronouns to imply a commonality between author
and readership ('our national history' [xi], for example) which runs
counter to his decision to abridge his epic and publish it only in English.
However, it appears that Kunene is attempting to exploit the tension
between a notional or implied Zulu audience and an actual international
readership in presenting Shaka as a leader with specific national
valencies in the African subcontinent, but worthy of symbolic stature
amongst great leaders worldwide. This dual purpose of the poem is
reflected in Kunene's translation strategy: 'I have eliminated the colonial
terminology like "hut", "chief", "headman", etc., and, rather, based my
terminology on corresponding terms in the two societies [European/
English and Zulu]. I have projected the concept of power as defined by the
society in question and as historically comparable with the concepts of a
similar society under similar circumstances' (xxvii).[4]

Kunene's ideas about the role of poetry are clearly derived from his
sense of the function of oral literature in Zulu society: he says 'it interprets, focuses and analyses the past as well as the present and then creates
a perspective on the future', arguing that 'the previous generation, the
present generation, and the future generation [constitute] ... an integrated
whole' (Barnett 1983: 104). Further, he stresses that oral literature is
meant 'not merely to entertain but primarily to teach social values and
serious philosophical concepts' (ibid.: 105). Copies of the English translation of *Emperor Shaka the Great* were in fact circulated to ANC guerillas
in the training camps in the hope that the poem would give them a sense
of renewed strength and selfhood.[5] As a central part of his project of
asserting the importance of African cultural traditions, Kunene locates
himself and his poem firmly within oral literary forms and institutions.
He stresses that his poem derives from oral historical sources, and claims
for these an authenticity and veracity which directly oppose apartheid/
Bantu Education accounts and Social-Darwinist perceptions of oral
societies. In addition, in listing amongst its sources '[h]ighly trained
national historians (*abalandi bezindaba zabadala*)', '[m]y uncle, A
Ngcobo' and my 'great, great grandmother' , Kunene appears concerned to
construct a 'history from below' (though I shall return to this point later in
considering Haynes' critique of Kunene on this account). He emphasises
the education he received in indigenous literary expression and exegesis
from his parents,[6] and insists that he himself has been 'chosen' as a writer
in the way that an *imbongi* or praise poet would have been; that what he
produces does not come from himself, but is channelled through him in
some kind of prophetic/visionary way. Kunene's account of his beginning
to write suggests the very real continuities he wishes to draw, and which
he clearly feels very deeply, between writing and ancestral or spiritual
guidance. He links the childhood stirrings of poetry within him to the
sun: 'My home was on a hill or mountain overlooking the ocean, a very
spectacular place, so I used to look at the sun as it came out of the ocean

and it was so fantastic. I didn't know what to do about it, it just troubled me. And then it came, it just happened, there was no plan' (Wilkinson 1992: 137). And his more conscious literary production, his writing, has involved linking the symbol of literacy – the table – with that of ancestral guidance – the sun: 'When I started writing, my father brought me a small table, a folding table, so that I could go round the house. In the morning I would write on one side, facing the sun ... then move and face the other way, always following the sun' (Wilkinson 1992:138). In the sense of having been 'chosen' as a literate *imbongi*, he sees himself as being in a direct line with the great Zulu poet of the nineteenth century, Magolwane, whom he describes as 'one of the greatest of African poets, indeed I would say one of the greatest world poets' (Goodwin 1982: 178). He has himself claimed that, though he understands and accepts the benefits of the printed word, he wishes people not to read his poem but to perform it (Wilkinson 1992:139).

Kunene describes the praise poems (*izibongo*) of the king as 'elevating the highest desirable qualities in society', and as 'project[ing] an ethical system beyond the circumstances of the individual' (xxix). Goodwin points to the changes in the tradition of praising brought about by Magolwane: 'To Magolwane [Kunene] ascribes a revolution in Zulu poetry, including the introduction of political and social analysis, penetration of character, philosophical ideas, and abundant imagery (notably of ferocious animals)' (1982:178). Kunene's poem provides vivid accounts of praising:

> The poet celebrated the occasion with these poems,
> Speaking slowly, not throwing away his words.
> He danced leisurely, turning his body in circles.
> He moved gracefully, eager to exhibit his skill.
> Even his tuft of feathers waved gently like branches in the wind. (65–6)

and:

> Yet none could surpass in skill Magolwane,
> Who was the beautiful voice of the Ancestral Spirit.
> He scattered words like sparks of fire.
> He beat the ground with his ceremonial stick.
> His voice trembled and boomed to the cliffs. (174–5)

And it offers some truly memorable translations of the praises of Shaka recorded by James Stuart. More fundamentally, though, *Emperor Shaka the Great* incorporates into its own textuality – into its own structure of feeling – the strategies of praising, particularly those introduced by Magolwane (the extended praise, the Shakan stanza, and so on):

> Angered, they marched on Khali of the emaMbatheni clan.
> They hurried to Ndonda of the Deep River;
> They attacked Nyanya of the Great Dlamini clan.
> They danced high, showing off their invincible weapons. (61)

Hence at a fundamental textual level, the recuperation of tradition and the validation – even valorisation – of Zuluness are woven into Kunene's poem. *Emperor Shaka the Great* also stresses the importance of *izibongo* as a means of political criticism, particularly in the dramatic intervention of the praise poet in pulling Shaka out of his torpor following the death of his mother Nandi and the destruction caused by the enforced period of mourning (344ff.). There is probably no better text than *Emperor Shaka the Great* to suggest the extent of praising in Zulu society. As well as praising, other forms of Zulu expression are used in the poem, including prayers and songs of place, such as the following:

> Unto this day those who pass there sing the ancient songs.
> They hear the voices of the dead as they wash their feet.
> They implore the Ancestors to sing with them.
> The great Zululand shall rise again! (357)

Kunene's poem is subtitled a 'Zulu epic'. There is much debate about the validity of the concept of the 'African epic', which could occupy the entire space of an article, so I do not wish to engage with this question here.[7] Let it suffice to say that Kunene regards *izibongo*, particularly in their expanded form following the developments of poets like Magol-wane, with other forms including historical narratives, as comprising an epic tradition which expressed 'dramatic national events' (xxv–xxvi). He refers constantly in his own poem to praise poems as being 'heroic' or 'ancestral epics', and it is clear that Kunene sees his own epic as being in direct line with the 'epics' (*izibongo*) of Magolwane.

The function of these epics is closely linked with the creation of a national symbolism and founding mythology, and is thus very close, as several critics have noted, to Western definitions of the epic. The definition offered by M. H. Abrams in *A Glossary of Literary Terms* could apply equally to Kunene's poem:

> In its strict use by literary critics the term epic or heroic poem is applied to a work that meets at least the following criteria: it is a long narrative poem on a great and serious subject, related in an elevated style, and centred on a heroic or quasi-divine figure on whose actions depend the fate of a tribe, a nation, or the human race. The 'traditional epics' (also called 'primary epics' or 'folk epics') were shaped by a literary artist from historical or legendary materials which had developed in the oral traditions of his people during a period of expansion or warfare. (1971: 50).

And so from the table, as opposed to the sun, and particularly the desk in California rather than the table in Zululand, come the echoes of Virgil and Homer (stressed by the diction of Kunene's translation). Textually, Kunene's poem shares many features with Western epics, including the use of set passages or 'formulae' as described by Milman Parry and Albert Lord in relation to Homer,[8] scenes of feasting and one-to-one combat, descriptions of battles, direct interventions by the gods in human affairs, prophecy, and so on. One example may suffice. After her abandonment by

Shaka's father Senzangakhona, his mother Nandi is described in terms which echo Dido's predicament after discovering that Aeneas is planning to leave her:

> Hallucinations of horrendous snakes writhed around her.
> They bound up her ribs; they put knots in her voice.
> She began to lose her sanity, shouting the name of her lover.
> She called his name; he did not answer -
> Only the echoes came bounding from the distant cliffs.
> In her madness she heard footsteps
> As if echoing from passing crowds. (8)

As well as suggesting correspondences between epic forms across societies and historical periods (which we should not simply dismiss because they sit uncomfortably with current emphases on historicisation), these echoes may be part of Kunene's project of establishing Shaka as an epic hero worthy of international reputation; and they clearly fit with the emphasis in Negritude, not on rejecting the West, but on selectively reincorporating it and reinterpreting it along 'African' lines - of setting African and Western forms, and figures, beside each other as mutually influential and beneficial. This line of argument would explain the other European influences evident in Kunene's portrayal of a leader who is at once the Zulu founding figure, an African hero, and a great human leader: those of Shakespeare and of Christianity. Kunene has described similarities (though also differences) between what he refers to as the 'nationalism' of the Elizabethan court and that of Zulu society under Shaka (Duerden and Pieterse 1982: 86). Though, as Goodwin points out (1982:181), Kunene does not attribute Shaka's downfall to any hubris or flaw within his character (in fact the epic hardly deals with Shaka's psychological or spiritual state), several of his speeches echo those of Hamlet or Macbeth,[9] Kunene uses dramatic irony in the scene before Shaka's assassination in a way that parallels the analogous scene in *Julius Caesar*, and Princess Mkhabayi is presented as fulfilling a similar role to that of the witches in *Macbeth* (395–6). As regards Christian influences, Senzangakhona's attempts to kill the child Shaka echo Herod's Murder of the Innocents, and the story about the generous man and the snuff has a Christ-like aspect (188).

But the 'structures of feeling' of township life in South Africa in the late 1960s and 1970s, particularly as a result of developments in Black Consciousness (BC), were far removed from the epic forms of Vergil and Homer, the tragic heroes of Shakespeare, or even the heroic *izibongo* of Magolwane. Though Black Consciousness did valorise leaders such as Shaka, it did so in a rhetoric – through a structure of feeling – of the ghetto and the street. Mongane Serote's famous poem 'City Johannesburg' (1972), for example, gathers force from its ironic distance from the forms of epic praising – the salute is a search for a passbook, not a '*Bayete*' to the king – and Ingoapele Madingoane's 'black trial' (1979) is a Brechtian or Black

Power epic, rather than a heroic Homeric narrative. As Mothobi Mutloatse said in his famous statement on BC attitudes to form:

> We will have to donder conventional literature: old-fashioned critic and reader alike. We are going to have to pee, spit and shit on literary convention before we are through, we are going to kick, push and drag literature into the form we prefer. We are going to experiment and probe and not give a damn what the critics have to say. Because we are in search of our true selves – undergoing self-discovery as a people.
>
> We are not going to be told how to re-live our feelings, pains and aspirations by anyone who speaks from the platform of his own rickety culture. (1980: 5)

Kunene's poem is far removed from such aggressive, 'modern' assertions, and Malaba's dismissal of *Emperor Shaka the Great* as merely a 'throwback to the slogan Black is Beautiful' (1988: 477) seems entirely to miss the point. Kunene's poem is fundamentally out of touch with the rhetoric of Black Consciousness.[10] It seems to me that the lack of response to Kunene's poem in South Africa (Sitas complains of its being 'largely unread' even in KwaZulu Natal (1994: 151)) is less because of its banning (which did not prevent other texts from achieving popularity and influence through covert distribution), than because, from his position in exile, Kunene was removed from the structure of feeling of his South African audience. His project may have accorded with the Africanist agendas of the US – the hagiography of the institutions of African tradition and history. But the poem's lofty diction; the curious timelessness and placelessness of its Western epic evocations; its promotion of 'tribal' influences and forms and its use of Zulu in the original – which were viewed with suspicion by BC activists as potentially reinforcing the social divisions of apartheid; its remove from the cut and thrust of political mobilisation and the exigencies of evading police surveillance and interrogation; all made it seem contradictory, anachronistic and distant.

As Williams suggests, 'ways of talking' are bound up with 'ways of feeling', and the formal ambiguities of Kunene's poem are matched by the ambiguities of his presentation of Shaka; the power and compulsion of Shaka as a great and heroic leader (and here the poet achieves great success) yet the contradictions of the poem's 'ethnic' and 'national' sympathies. In contrast to colonial and apartheid assertions of Shaka's unprecedented brutality, Kunene presents him as a wise, democratic ruler and a supreme military tactician. He emphasises particularly Shaka's intellectual abilities, including his 'scientific methods' (77), and his capabilities as diplomat and statesman (skills he inherited and refined from Dingiswayo). While accounts of Shaka's innovative methods of warfare are well-known,[11] Kunene insists that amongst Shaka's greatest achievements were both the democratisation of society, in the sense that the holding of public office was no longer tied to clan membership or family history, and the construction of a powerful national ideology: 'to be a Zulu no longer signified merely clan membership or family position, but a political grouping whose composition was inter-family and international' (xx).

In accomplishing the creation of the Zulu nation, Shaka is presented as fulfilling the prophecies of his own, and his people's, destiny. From the outset there are references to 'the birthplace of our nation' (2), so that the personal destiny/greatness of Shaka and Zulu nationalism are closely linked from the start. Shaka's power is evident even in childhood: 'But Shaka of the tiger never bowed his head./All feared his anger./Even those who claimed the authority of age retreated from him' (29). And almost all of the important characters foresee Shaka's greatness. His mother Nandi says:

> I knew one day my son would grow to overshadow the earth.
> He shall tower high above all living beings.
> The little mites that mocked us shall tremble before him.
> They shall say: 'Shaka is fearful. Shaka strikes
> But no one dares to strike him back'. (22)

His father Senzangakhona says, 'Everywhere I look I see a vision of my son Shaka' (34); and even Princess Mkhabayi in plotting his assassination says:

> In truth, Shaka's power can never be destroyed.
> It will emerge in the hearts of many generations.
> They shall make their sacrifice of the black bull in his name. (421)

Shaka's destiny to build the Zulu nation is presented in the poem especially through symbolic visions of the greatness of the 'Palm Race',[12] and this destiny is to be fulfilled because of Shaka's innovative qualities of leadership and commitment to the national ideal above all else:

> He knew, too, that Shaka was like the wind
> Which often lies low at dawn
> But, stirred by the feet of men, leaps up to the heavens;
> Yet by sunset it falls again quietly on the ground.
> Such was the temperament of the great ruler of the Zulus.
> No sign or symbol or emblem was sacred to him;
> Only order and the eternal visions for the Palm race. (365–6)

Shaka reveals himself, in Kunene's poem, to be concerned particularly with discursive constructions of nationalism, which echoes Kunene's own project in offering his poetic account of the ruler. The narrator says explicitly, 'kingdoms and states are kept intact by their poets /It is they who embellish their tales, making the future desirable' (168). Later in the poem he[13] links such poetic performances directly with nationalism: 'The utterances of poets are like prayers to the Ancestors./The era of greatness flourishes with the epics of the nations' (246), and more directly, 'A nation's power lies in its weapons and poems' (272). Shaka himself says, 'Zulu power no longer issues from conquest/ But from a bond of an all-embracing nationhood' (199), and he affirms, 'all nations are made powerful by their rituals' (305). Indeed, many accounts of the performances of poems or songs echo the unisonality described by Benedict Anderson (1983) in the construction of imagined national communities. After a performance of praise songs following a military victory, for example, the narrator affirms: 'Such were the songs that cemented the bonds of clans and nations' (177).

Notions of national identity, particularly in their overt creation and manipulation, have been the subject of criticism from a variety of positions, notably by postcolonial scholars. Yet we should acknowledge that Kunene's poem comes out of a context of social and discursive rupture, with political structures and cultural institutions and forms having been violently torn apart. So Shaka's, and Kunene's, overt nationalism and cultural assertion may be seen to be historically necessary. This is clearly Ursula Barnett's understanding when she says:

> This is not an academic or chauvinistic attempt at historical or heroic preservation, but an imaginative interpretation of African philosophy. Kunene tries to replace what Black South Africa lost under conquest: the feeling for the continuity of history, not as an object lesson for modern times, not as stimulus to nostalgia and pride, but as part of one's life. He demonstrates how we live in the past and present, and thus shape our future. (1983:108)

Malaba's critique of Kunene for 'presenting [the reader] with a demigod, not a human being' (1988: 483), published nine years after Kunene's poem in very different historical circumstances, seems to me – despite its claimed awareness of Black Consciousness and Africanist debates – insufficiently cognisant of the pressures of the time. Instead, Malaba seems to fall back on a rather curious empiricism, stating that Kunene is simply 'wrong' in not making Shaka more brutal, etc., claims which are difficult, if not impossible, to substantiate.

In her statement quoted above, though, Barnett appears to gloss over certain real difficulties in the poem. Haynes, for example, is worried particularly that Kunene's epic is very much a 'history from above' (1987: 56), and he talks of the 'commentary-box view of battle scenes' (ibid.: 57). He links this criticism with the larger problem within the poem's nationalist agenda: its contradictory endorsements of Zulu and African nationalisms.

Kunene's own position both as an ANC activist/leader and a staunch supporter of the Zulu royal family is a vexed one (though Nelson Mandela reveals similarly dual allegiances in relation to Xhosa society). In the preface Kunene says: 'I thank particularly my brother and leader, Prince Gatsha Buthelezi, who greatly inspired and encouraged me. His glorious example of leadership is a true continuation of the tradition of his ancestor, Shaka the Great himself' (xi). This is not in itself reason to criticise Kunene for ideological contradiction, for Buthelezi was himself a member of the ANC prior to forming Inkatha in 1975, and at least two other studies, clearly not supportive of Inkatha's separatist agenda, contain dedications to Buthelezi.[14] However, the poem itself makes numerous references to the greatness of the Kunene and Buthelezi clans ('Phungashe was the powerful king of the Buthelezi nation' (56), 'There came the powerful Buthelezis of the House of Shenge' (305)), and celebrates the institutions of Zulu kingship so anxiously presided over by Inkatha (and antipathetic to Black Consciousness activists and thinkers). Kunene also assumes in the poem a basic Zulu ethic, which gives spiritual and moral weight to the notion of Zuluness. While this ethic is contrasted vividly with the stupidity, greed and arrogance displayed by the white settlers, and so becomes an effective means of political protest on Kunene's behalf, it also promotes 'tribal' understandings and divisions. And this despite the fact that Kunene wishes in the poem to 'pay tribute to all the African martyrs from Algeria to South Africa who have shared the great dream of a great Africa for all her children' (xxii), and has the narrator make statements in the poem such as 'They acclaim the swiftness in battle of the iziChwe regiment./ It is truly the shield and spear of the nation' (74), which undeniably calls to mind the military wing of the ANC, *Umkhonto we Sizwe*, the 'Spear of the Nation'. Haynes sees in Kunene's royalist sympathies a distressing trend:

> Whatever contradictions we might discern in Kunene's adherence to both the ANC and to Buthelezi, it does seem that the ideological trend in *Emperor Shaka the Great* is towards bringing the immediate struggles against apartheid under the wider sway of the Zulu ruling family, or, by extension, some form of 'top-down' populism under a charismatic 'great leader', a further 'embellishment' and 'mythification', no doubt. And this would be a 'long-term national and social goal'. To most Africans, especially those on the left, it is an ominous and familiar scenario. (1987: 61)

As Ari Sitas points out, Kunene is an easy target for criticism in respect of his 'ethnic' and 'national' ambivalences:

> Of course he offers an easy target for people who are against the revival of Zulu ethnicity as a foundation stone for homeland independence, and his work could be used for such conservative ends. Despite treading such danger-zones, his work is larger than that: it is, according to him 'a cosmic address, a prayer to life, a celebration of the great accomplishments of man'. (1994:143)

Perhaps the ease of such judgements should give us pause, and Sitas is correct in pointing to the larger implications of the work. In suggesting that the generation and reception of Kunene's poem reflect disparate structures of feeling, I am attempting to move beyond the simple dichotomy of hagiography or rejection/impassivity of critical responses to Kunene, to serious analysis of the poem and its readings. Perhaps Kunene's poem should be set alongside other texts, and prominent figures, who reveal similar kinds of 'ethnic' and 'national' affiliations. In *Long Walk to Freedom*, Mandela describes the effect upon himself of a performance by the great Xhosa *imbongi*, S. E. K. Mqhayi: 'I felt such intense pride at that point, not as an African, but as a Xhosa: I felt like one of the chosen people' (1995: 49). Yet when he describes a performance of the praises of Shaka, his emphasis is very different: 'Suddenly there were no Xhosas or Zulus, no Indians or Africans, no rightists or leftists, no religious or political leaders; we were all nationalists and patriots bound together by a love of our common history, our culture, our country and our people' (1995: 235). Certainly modern identity politics, particularly in South Africa, involve layers and webs of competing and often conflicting allegiance. Perhaps the value of a poem like Kunene's is that critical discussion of it allows us to stage such debates openly: asking difficult questions, while allowing the symbolic power and resonance of identificatory mythologies.

We may also ask whether the poem – perhaps particularly through its elevated epic form, which suggests the possibility of symbolic resolutions – may have meanings now which would not have been open to readers in the 1970s? Are the contradictory structures of feeling capable of more productive interaction now? Are we reminded – in South Africa – of the way in which different lines of continuity – in fact different structures of feeling – have run through our history, and continue to swirl together in the complexity of the present? Are we perhaps reminded that – despite the overwhelming claims of BC in the 1970s, its aggressive pushing of all else to the side – the current leaders, at least partly because they were physically removed from society by imprisonment or exile, need to be understood in terms of the kind of heroic Africanist rhetoric that Kunene represents. Nelson Mandela and Thabo Mbeki – especially in the latter's calls for an African Renaissance – in many ways represent the continuing structure of feeling, including its ethnic/national contradictions, that Kunene's poem expresses. Mandela in particular has emphasised his connections with the rural world of custom and tradition, and we may remember that, in contrast, Black Consciousness remained a largely urban phenomenon. Perhaps *Emperor Shaka the Great,* with its accounts of life removed from the urban and industrial centre, may serve as a corrective to the urban bias in South African historiography, pointing to a sense of rural life and identification which has continued to exist, and which continues to assert its presence.

Whatever the problems and contradictions of the poem, I think Sitas's reminder of Kunene's larger accomplishments and concerns, quoted earlier, remains crucial. Kunene's (African/Zulu/South African/human?) assertion of the interconnectedness of life – of the spiritual and moral obligations to others and to the future – is a rebuke and a challenge to a society which is rapidly abandoning the politics of reconstruction for individual enrichment and material acquisition. As Kunene himself put it in another poem:

we are not the driftwood of distant oceans
our kinsmen are a thousand centuries old
only a few nations begat civilization
not of gold, not of things but of people (quoted in Sitas 1994: 143).

Perhaps this fundamental assumption – this assertion – of human inter-dependence is the true structure of feeling of Kunene's poem.

NOTES

1. See Hamilton (1998) and Wylie (1999) for detailed analysis of some of the conflicting images of Shaka.
2. Kunene claims the veracity of his representation over that of Thomas Mofolo ('My *Shaka* is more historical. Mofolo's is just myth' (Wilkinson, 1992:140)) and others ('So my *Shaka* is more authentic, definitely' (ibid.:141)).
3. An incomplete version of the Zulu manuscript (comprising about two-thirds of the epic) is presently lodged in the Campbell Collections, University of Natal, Durban. A detailed comparative analysis of this manuscript with Kunene's English translation, which is beyond my abilities as critic, needs to be undertaken. A superficial comparison suggests that the Zulu and English texts are indeed rather different.
4. This strategy does not always seem to me successful. Kunene's use of terms like 'foreign potentate' (65) or 'gangster kings' (103) sometimes risks historical incongruity or anachronism.
5. Personal communication with the author.
6. He says about the literary education he received from his parents: 'So there was a kind of very deep critique of how you put things in a language. Literature was very important: it was not just literature for its own sake, it was history, politics, the philosophy of society and everything. So through history and through literature they were training their own children about various aspects of life including ethics' (Wilkinson, 1992: 138).
7. See Upland (1984) for discussion of these debates.
8. Some examples of these formulae include: 'The dawn was the brilliant eye of morning' (20); 'Dawn speared eternally from the horizon' (34); 'The delicate scent of meat rose in waves to the heavens' (80); and 'the morning came, with her children, from the mountains' (221).
9. It is unclear to what extent the echoes of *Macbeth* are a result of Kunene's familiarity with the Zulu stage production of *Macbeth*, *Umabatha* (first performed in 1970).
10. Ari Sitas makes an analogous point: 'The result is a poetry dislocated from the immediate stuctures of feeling and the rhythms of resistance of a modern day industrial proletariat ...' (1994: 146).
11. Wylie (1999), however, argues that accounts of Shaka's innovative methods of warfare, particularly the introduction of the stabbing spear, have little evidentiary basis.
12. Kunene argues that 'Palm Race' is a mythological appellation for the Zulu nation, signify-ing – through the image of a single tree with many trunks – multiplicity within a broader unity (personal communication with the author).
13. Notwithstanding the poem's reliance in its sources on women's oral testimony, within Kunene's patriarchal social conception the narrator is clearly male.
14. See Liz Gunner's doctoral thesis *'Ukubonga Nezibongo:* Zulu Praising and Praises' (1984) and Jeff Guy's *The Destruction of the Zulu Kingdom* (1979).

WORKS CITED

Abrams, M H., *A Glossary of Literary Terms*, New York: Holt, Reinhart & Winston, 1981.

Anderson, Benedict, *Imagined Communities*, London: Verso, 1991 (1983).

Barnett, Ursula A., *A Vision of Order: A Study of Black South African Literature in English (1914–1980)*, London: Sinclair Browne; Amherst: University of Massachusetts Press and Cape Town: Maskew Miller Longman, 1983.

Brown, Duncan, 'Interview with Mongane Wally Serote', *Theoria* 80 (October): 143–9, 1992.

Dorsey, David, 'Critical Perception of African Poetry', *African Literature Today* 16, 1988.

Duerden, Denis and Pieterse, Cosmo (eds), *African Writers Talking*, London: Heinemann, 1982.

Gérard. Albert S., *African Language Literatures*, Harlow: Longman, 1981.

Goodwin, Ken, *Understanding African Poetry*, London: Heinemann, 1982.

Gunner, Liz, *'Ukubonga Nezibongo:* Zulu Praising and Praises'. DPhil. Thesis, School of Oriental and African Studies, University of London, 1984.

Guy, Jeff, *The Destruction of the Zulu Kingdom*, Pietermaritzburg: University of Natal Press, 1994 (1979).

Hamilton, Carolyn, *Terrific Majesty: The Powers of Shaka Zulu and the Limits of the Historical Imagination*, Cape Town: David Philip, 1998.

Haynes, John, *African Poetry and the English Language*, London: Macmillan, 1987.

Kunene, Mazisi, *Zulu Poems*, London: Deutsch, 1970.

—— *Emperor Shaka the Great: A Zulu Epic*, London: Heinemann, 1979.

—— *Anthem of the Decades*, London: Heinemann, 1981.

—— *The Ancestors and the Sacred Mountain*, London: Heinemann, 1982.

Madingoane, Ingoapele, *africa my beginning*, Johannesburg: Ravan, 1979.

Malaba, Mbongeni Z., 'Super-Shaka: Mazisi Kunene's *Emperor Shaka the Great*', *Research in African Literatures* 19(4) (Winter), 1988: 477–88.

Mandela, Nelson, *Long Walk to Freedom*, London: Abacus, 1995 (1994).

Mutloatse, Mothobi (ed.), *Forced Landing*, Johannesburg: Ravan, 1980.

Opland, Jeff, 'The Transition from Oral to Written Literature: Areas of Research into South African Bantu Languages' in: Charles Malan (ed). *SA Literature Research*, Pretoria: HSRC, 1984.

Serote, Mongane Wally, *Yakhal'inkomo*, Johannesburg: Renoster, 1972.

Sesay, Kodiatu, 'Hopes of a Harvest Festival', *African Literature Today* 16, 1988.

Sitas, Ari, 'Traditions of Poetry in Natal' in Liz Gunner (ed.), *Politics and Performance: Theatre, Poetry and Song in Southern Africa*, Johannesburg: Witwatersrand University Press, 1994: 139–61.

Wilkinson, Jane, *Talking with African Writers*, London: James Currey and Portsmouth, NH: Heinemann, 1992.

Williams, Raymond, *The Long Revolution*, New York: Columbia University Press, 1961.

Wylie, Dan, *Savage Delight*, Pietermaritzburg: University of Natal Press, 1999.

Popular Songs & Social Realities
in Post-Independence Zimbabwe

M. T. Vambe

During the Zimbabwean liberation struggle of the 1970s, the degree to which a song became 'popular' depended on the African community's acceptance of the values of national self-assertion and a quest for political freedom which the African singers sang about. But after independence African singers produce, circulate and receive songs under broadened market situations and are struggling to maintain a 'local' market in a context in which global influences are dominant. Consequently like other aspects of popular culture such as local film, television and theatre, songs protest or resist in a contradictory manner, for they are already implicated in the status quo (Gecau in Wilkins 1996: 22). In the early 1980s in Zimbabwe, what made African songs by African singers 'popular' was the way the songs captured and celebrated the happy mood of independence. But beneath this spirit of celebrating independence were intense struggles by the state to control, reshape and reorganise the orientation of popular singers so as to prevent them from realising the full implications of their messages on the need for social justice. Popular singers' responses to the state's efforts to manipulate them were not uniform as they tended to acquiesce, resist and incorporate some nationalist elite values into their songs, and even negotiate meanings with more powerful groups all at once, so that the ground on which popular singers met with the dominant nationalist ideology resulted in the emergence of a negotiated version of independence in the songs. Although the songs of the late 1980s and 1990s attempted to 'name' reality in ways that more openly interrogate and oppose 'official truths and accounts' of both the war and independence, even when the songs reveal an awareness of uneven forms of consciousness among the rank and file of the masses themselves, the 'mobile combinations' (Bennett in Storey 1994: 225) of contradictory responses in the voices of the popular singers suggest that popular songs in post-independence Zimbabwe are not the cultural sites where people's values are simplistically either deformed by the ruling elites or their authenticity asserted by the subordinate classes.

Song, patronage, the state and ideology

At the height of the Zimbabwean war the major sources of popular songs were the Home artists, singing about the war from inside the country, and the guerrillas using songs as media for communicating war aims in the process of conscientising the masses. (Pongweni 1982).

However, in the refugee camps such as Chimoio and Tembgwe in Mozambique, and Mgagao in Tanzania, the nationalist leadership commissioned singers to sing about the centrality of the leaders in the war. The leaders presented the masses as an amorphous body of unthinking humanity who followed in the footsteps of those who led them. This helped create the myth which set the leaders as superior to and apart from the ordinary men and women. While the leaders took themselves as the think-tanks of the struggle and the ordinary people as gullible masses, this was presented to the same masses in such a way that it did not disturb but reinforced the other war myth that the wishes/aspirations of the leaders were the same as those of the people at the grassroots (Chiwome in Spencer-Walters 1998: 154).

At independence in 1980 the nationalist government was still determined to control and redirect the content of popular songs towards praising the leaders for organising, executing, winning the war and 'freeing' the masses from colonial bondage. The state tended to infiltrate and manipulate those groups of oral singers which depended on it for financial support. For example, the Zimbabwe African National Liberation Army (ZANLA) Choir which during the struggle had been the ideological and cultural arm of the military wing of ZANLA forces, had its role significantly reorganised after independence. In the early 1980s the ZANLA Choir graced state occasions such as Independence Day Celebrations. Only those songs which projected the nationalist government's outlook were allowed to be played on the state-controlled Radio two station in the country. But the situation tended to be different regarding the relationship of the state to well-established singers such as Thomas Mapfumo and Oliver Mtukudzi. These singers had been around in the 1970s. Their popularity owed little to state backing. Mapfumo and Mtukudzi owned the band instruments they used and therefore had some 'free' space to sing songs which both celebrated independence as well as question certain state policies. But, even these 'independent' singers were aware in the 1980s of the need for political patronage from the state. Consequently, sometimes they would compose songs that outright praised the new leadership even when the singers did not benefit materially from the state. One way of explaining this seeming contradictory position of popular singers could be that certain of their views and hopes of what independence should bring coincided with those of the leaders. Perhaps, as Stuart Hall reminds us, the relationship between the state and popular artists cannot always be plotted on a narrow dialectic suggested by the double movement of containment and resistance. Sometimes popular artists become complicit by virtue of recognising certain elements of identification with state policies, 'something approaching a re-creation of recognisable experiences and attitudes [to] which people are responding'(Hall in Storey 1994: 461).

A further complicating factor in the state's relationship to popular artists in the 1980s was the contradictory role of recording companies. On the one hand the mood of independence tended to put pressure on these companies to make records of songs that more or less reproduced the officially acceptable account of the history of the war and its aftermath. On the other hand, the companies claimed that they did not interfere with the singers' lyrics (Zindi 1985: 67). It is however difficult to say whether or not the companies ever accepted completely the state policies of patronising popular artists. But what seems clear is that the companies also needed a stable market, which to some extent the state could politically guarantee. There was thus potential for the recording companies or cultural industries to constantly rework and reshape what they represented, and, by repetition and selection, to impose and implant certain meanings in the popular songs as might fit easily with the descriptions of the nationalists' preferred meanings.

Whether it was the oral artists or the well-established singers now with their own instruments yet harnessing new forms of technology, the relationship between the artists and the recording companies was not always amicable. The latter tended to maximise profit at the expense of the singers who in most cases received 5 to 10 per cent as royalties for the sale of each single (Zindi 1985: 65). But because recording companies desired to maintain their markets, they could let certain record discs whose messages castigated state officials pass through. Thus while the companies could promote 'subversive' songs to boost sales, they also took care not to antagonise the state. Although it is not easy to totally capture all the reasons which motivated recording companies to promote some 'subversive' singers on one hand and not anger the state on the other, we would generally agree with Stuart Hall who argues that capital's concern in popular culture is to reorganise it in ways which not only imply struggle and resistance but also incorporation, appropriation and expropriation as well (Hall in Storey 1994: 463).

So. the uneven struggles between the state, the recording companies and the popular artists in the early 1980s waged within the conflicting activities of strategic lines of 'alliances as well as lines of cleavages' (Hall in Storey 1994: 456) had far-reaching consequences on popular songs. For example, in the context of newly-won independence, the song 'Zuva Ranhasi' ('The day of Independence') by the ZANLA Choir reminded the peasants of the significant contribution of Nehanda, Chaminuka and Tongogara in inspiring the masses to fight colonialism. But the frequency with which 'Zuva Ranhasi' was played on Radio two suggested something more than simply celebrating independence. Whether or not the DJs at Mbare Studios were aware of it, 'Zuva Ranhasi' tended to legitimise the rule of the nationalist leaders. The song projects the war as having been fought by one ethnic group, the Shona people who make up 70 per cent of the population of Zimbabwe, and from whom most of the powerful leaders of the new government originated. In the process of the state's re-writing of 'national' history, 'Zuva Ranhasi' portrayed Robert Mugabe's pre-dominantly Shona-based ZANU government as a natural and indisputable political heir to the Shona ancestral leaders of the past. In the song, other political parties such as ZAPU, with a broad-based following among the Ndebele people and which also participated in the war, are excluded. Thus, while 'Zuva Ranhasi' attempts to embody the 'national' spirit of celebrating the attaining of independence, the same song nevertheless encourages anti-pluralistic tendencies in political thinking in Zimbabwe.

Another political strategy used by the state to neutralise the power of popular song was to instruct the state-controlled radio stations in the country to withdraw from the shelves those songs which appeared subversive of state policies. Following the government's introduction of the policy of reconciliation in the 1980s, some songs such as 'Maruza Imi Vapambeptumi!' ('You have lost, you white oppressors'), which during the struggle ridiculed whites. had to be withdrawn from the air. The state argued that these songs could foment social discord and threatened to undermine the government's policy of reconciliation which, as poor blacks had already begun to see, was a major scandal of betrayal (Victor de Waal 1992: 62) because the policy left the economy virtually in the hands of former white Rhodesians. In place of politically subversive songs, the state encouraged popular artists to sing songs that evoked 'love' and 'patriotism' towards one's country. But the terms 'love' and 'patriotism' were never defined in concrete ways. Some oral artists fell into the trap of the state's propaganda. Songs such as 'Thando' ('Love') and 'Be Zimbabwe Masithandane' ('Zimbabweans let's love one another') reflect the state's thinking that the views of private persons, civic groups and other political parties that oppose those of the government are necessarily subversive and therefore retard development. In particular, 'Be Zimbabwe Masithandane' encourages a monolithic vision of a new society in which the leaders have a common destiny with the masses despite the sharp differences in the standard of living between the two social groups in the country.

> Comradeship is the greatest asset. Discord tears our country apart. Our salvation is in building our country on love ... Malcontents will have us forget this.

Those specifically defined by the state as political 'malcontents' in the 1980s were the ZAPU combatants who refused to lay down their guns in the government's spirit of reconciliation. It is ironical that Thomas Mapfumo, who in the struggle had earned his title as the 'Chimurenga

Guru' for singing against oppression, was in the 1980s joining government officials in castigating the so-called 'dissidents'. Mapfumo's song,
'Chigwindiri' ('The feigned brave one') projects the ZAPU fighters as purposeless rebels, who have to be decimated by the government forces.
Mapfumo's other song 'Nyaya Huru' ('The big story') went further to
elevate Robert Mugabe as the 'father' of Zimbabwe. Implied in 'Nyaya
Huru' is that, as a father-figure, the new prime minister's political activities are above censure. Here are some lines from the song;

> Mugabe is the big cock here
> All the masses are happy
> The troubles we saw in the struggle
> Were finished by Mugabe.

While the leader is portrayed as invincible, the masses are gullible, don't
know what they want, and have to be 'freed' from colonial bondage. What
is being erected is the myth of the personality cult. This image of a
superior leader is, however, at odds with the democratic principle of
equality popularised during the struggle.

However, some singers such as Paul Matavire would – against the
background of the state's 'socialist' policies on health, education and land
– use their songs to question why the majority of people still lived in
abject poverty. In 'Dhiabhurosi Nyoka' ('Satan the Serpent'), Matavire
rejects the mythical explanation of poverty offered in the bible. He shows
that the widely accepted myth is sexist, anti-humanist and tenuous.
Matavire challenges the listener to find historical explanations for human
suffering (Chiwome in Spencer-Walters 1998: 157). In a similar vein,
Oliver Mtokudzi criticises the greed and avarice which now characterise
the private domain of love. In 'Nyanga yeNzou', ('The Elephant's Task'),
Mtukudzi shows how the marriage institution has turned mercenary with
fathers-in-law claiming exorbitant 'prizes' for their daughters. In a certain
sense, 'Nyanga yeNzou' criticises the individualism which has grown in the
rank and file of the ordinary people as well. In the 1990s Mtukudzi was,
through 'Chimbambaira' ('Sweet potato'), to bemoan the erosion of the
spirit of togetherness and sharing which characterised the liberation
struggle. In the songs of the late 1980s and 1990s, the contradictory
responses of the popular artists to hard times deepen although there is in
the songs a dominant sensibility of more open social protest in both their
content and form.

Songs and the re-negotiation of the meaning of Independence in the late 1980s and 1990s

The popular singers of the late 1980s and early 1990s were more concerned with deconstructing official truths about the process of nation-
building. Significant historical events in the late 1980s inspired the artists

to shift from a position of radical ambivalence towards independence to adopting a more open protestant ethic in the song, even when this response was fraught with its own contradictions. When the state sent the Sixth Brigade into Matebeleland to stem the tide of 'dissident' activities, the operation resulted in the loss of life of many Shona and Ndebele men and women. The state's military aggression towards its own people put into question the myth of collective destiny between the leaders and the people. The incident created an irreparable dent in credibility towards the state in the eyes of its electorate. Artists could no longer take the state for granted. The state was transformed into a material force that could go to the lengths of killing its 'own' people to consolidate its power. The desire of the state to suppress the discourse on ethnicity produced opposite results.

Singers such as Nicholas Zacharria questioned the state's frenzied denial of ethnic consciousness when, in actual fact, some political positions in government were granted on the basis of the ethnic origins of candidates. In 'Ndine Mubvunzo' ('I have a question') Zacharria speaks of the need for unity between 'tribal' groups in the country. The state through its control of Radio two, frequently pounced on the song, gave it more air play in order to justify the Unity Accord between the top ZANU and ZAPU politicians. But other singers such as the Bulawayo-based group Amabhubhesi were quick to point out that the unity accord represented the unity of political elites from the Shona and Ndebele groups. Ordinary people were left to suffer in the drought-stricken areas of Gwaai and Tsholotsho. In their song 'Jongwe naChikwari' ('The cock and Bateleur Eagle'), Amabhubhesi satirises the Ndebele political elites such as Dumiso Dabengwa who abandoned their own people and joined the ZANU government. In the song, 'Chikwari' who refuses to join the new government is praised, implying that the ordinary people are aware that the unity accord is a political sham meant to benefit the elites. Thus, the significance of the songs of Zacharria and Amabhubhesi helped to push the debate on ethnicity, nepotism and corruption on to the public domain, which the nationalist leaders had resisted during the struggle and after independence (Samupindi 1992).

With the increasing poverty of the rank and file, some artists felt that the state was not doing enough to promote them in the spirit of independence. Singers such as Susan Mapfumo and Zexie Manatsa were languishing in poverty without state help (Gunner 1994: 126) and other singers felt no obligation to promote the interests of a leadership which turned a blind eye to the plight of the ordinary people. As part of the contradictory growth and development of individual singers' consciousness, some popular singers like Thomas Mapfumo whose songs had praised the nationalist leaders in the early 1980s, began to dig in their heels in a process of soul searching about the true meaning of independence. In 'Maiti kurima Hamubvire' ('You used to say you are good farmers') Mapfumo bemoans the lost ideals of the struggle. The singer identifies the leaders as the cause of the failure of independence. Promises given to the masses on land, did not come to pass. In fact, funds donated by international organisations such as the World Bank in order to resettle landless peasants were diverted into the personal bank accounts of individual politicians. The measure of social decay and betrayal of independence ideals was the Willowgate scandal of 1989 in which high-ranking officials abused their power and acquired luxury cars cheaply only to sell them at exorbitant prices. Although the government of Robert Mugabe was to launch an inquiry, its sensitive results were suppressed. Mapfumo sang of the violation of the leadership code by the leaders themselves in 'Corruption'. In it, the moral decay of the leadership is revealed through the humiliation which women have to go through to get a job. Mapfumo sang that:

> The big fish are corrupt
> Some women strip for a job
> Everywhere, is corruption.

But even when Mapfumo's songs were trying to define a new role for the artist in the post-independence euphoria period of 1980 to 1985, the singer's vision never really succeeded in going beyond the ideological limitations of nationalism which his songs were attempting to interrogate. For example, in 'Varombo Kuvarombo', ('Poor people'), Mapfumo is still haunted by nationalism's unitary claims to collective destiny for the leaders and masses:

> The rulers of Rhodesia still possess the wealth ...
> But the government said it would promote cooperatives ...
> So that all of us should enjoy ...

Mapfumo still presents the post-independence social conflicts in terms of blacks versus whites. The singer makes a grudging acknowledgement that some rich blacks have joined some powerful whites in exploiting the subordinate classes. This is the sort of argument the state is comfortable with because it absolves its senior politicians of corrupt practices. In other words, the uneven levels of consciousness in Mapfumo's songs of the 1990s enable them to be manipulated by state officials in order to articulate official populist ideology. Because the singer fails to transcend the nationalist ideology he criticises, the song ends up moralising about the virtues of 'cooperatives', appealing to the moral conscience of the very leaders whose economic policies cause hardships in the lives of subordinate classes. This shows the weaknesses of a protest sensibility that has failed to transcend its own limitations.

But unlike singers of the older generation such as Mapfumo and Mtukudzi, the 1990s popular culture scenario in Zimbabwe has also seen the emergence of young singers many of whom were born after 1980. Young singers such as Leonard Zhakata have no illusions about independence. They were born into poverty and their songs catalogue the hardships of life under the 'infamous' Economic Structural Adjustment Programme. For Zhakata, poor men and women are hard-hit by poverty, especially in the urban centres. In 'Mugove' ('The Reward') the workers mourn the erosion of their incomes by incessant price increases. At work, the worker is given a meagre wage which is not enough for food and shelter. The voice of the complaining worker is strident:

> Can the elders give us chances
> So that I can warn those higher-up
> Those who trouble and spit on the poor
> I ask for my reward
> For I am being worn out by those with money
> Because I do not have anything for myself
> I am oppressed, over worked and abused.

But for Zhakata, it is the black leadership that has failed its people :

> If it was me in that position of leader
> I would call upon my people and say
> Come, let us share the fruits of independence.

It is significant to observe that Zhakata's songs such as 'Mugove' and 'Unochemeyi' ('Why do you cry?') attempt to push into the public arena a 'working class consciousness' which during the struggle was ruthlessly repressed by the nationalist leadership. Although the communal spirit of solidarity among the workers in 'Mugove' is not adequately worked through to demonstrate its revolutionary potential, implied in Zhakata's lyrics is the desire to demystify independence and show that the conflicting interests of social forces in post-independence Zimbabwe can no longer be obfuscated by vacuous rhetoric that appeals to national collective identities.

However, the ability of the young singers of the 1990s to point up the failure of the state's macroeconomic efforts does not necessarily suggest that they were aware of potentially viable solutions. For example, in 'Kumusha' ('Home') Michel Jambo and Tendai Mupfurutsa sing of the hard punches that the unemployed receive from hunger. In turn, the unemployed youth in the song decides to escape from the city and go to the rural areas. This rural area is depicted as a spiritual sanctuary untouched by the tentacles of the negative economic policies of the leaders. There is a romantic yearning for peace and material fulfilment which the voice in the song hungers for:

> ESAP has pitched me
> ESAP has throttled me
> I am running back to the rural
> areas where life is good.

Although the cities are focal points of capitalist forces, the rural areas in Zimbabwe have not been spared either. Instead of confronting the system, 'Kumusha' encourages escape. This tension at the heart of the song cannot, however, simply be described as an instance of false consciousness. It is a yearning for a fulfilling social existence even when its mode of response is to escape into another rural context defined by bitter struggles between capital and labour. The ambivalent responses to ESAP of the voice in 'Kumusha' can easily be misinterpreted as a product of a merely conservative impulse, backward-looking and anachronistic, while in actual fact it underscores the contradictory manner in which popular songs embody struggle and resistance but also incorporation, appropriation and expropriation by dominant power blocs.

Images of women in the popular songs of the 1990s

Part of the complex nature of popular songs in the 1990s is that they show a tendency to shift from public themes which one might term 'state politics' to comment on individual relationships between men and women within nuclear African families in both urban and rural areas. It is interesting to observe that most songs by male artists reveal a deep concern for society's need to control female sexuality. The major stereotypical images produced and circulated through most songs by male singers are those that present women as hopeless victims of social circumstances, dangerous and loose. As Gunner observed, female singers

> are seen as in some way even more outside the boundaries of areas of male control and the areas usually covered by 'wife', 'daughter', than other urban women and so, existing in unmarked territory, they are termed 'loose' or 'prostitute'. (Gunner 1994: 117)

A male singer such as Leonard Zhakata whose songs of political protest in the 1990s were instant hits seems, however, to portray women not only as victims of male machinations but also as objects of male sexual desire. In 'Maruva Enyika' ('The flowers of the country') the singer raises the important issue of AIDS that threatens humanity in Zimbabwe. For Zhakata, women are 'flowers' which decorate homes but the danger is that 'poison [AIDS] was poured in the "well" [female sexual organs] which is used by everybody'. Although it is generally poor women and children who have least access to information, to choices, and to health services, it is they who are taking the hardest punches in the struggle to beat the HIV challenges (McFadden in Meena 1992: 158). 'Maruva Enyika' gives the impression that women alone are the sufferers; women are depicted as victims but they are a 'dangerous' victim because they harbour the poison within them. The 'victims' approach (Gunner 1994: 114) in the portrayal of images of women in the popular songs is also present in Oliver Mtukudzi's 'Neria'. In it, a black woman is losing the property she has worked for with her late husband to unscrupulous sons-in-law. Although 'Neria' demonstrates the negative transformations of the institution of the extended family, the social processes responsible for these changes are reduced to the greediness of the late husband's male relatives. The selfishness and individualism that threaten 'Ukama' (extended family) are not linked to the social transformations occurring in the political public sphere. Consequently, this song encourages Nena and women in general to pray to God instead of educating women to have recourse to the legal courts to have the women protected by law:

> Neria, oh
> Do not be disheartened
> For God is with you
> You only have to be a morally strong woman

While 'Maruva Enyika' and 'Neria' attempt to be the ventriloquist for women's plight, the male singers' patriarchal perceptions of wanting to control women by projecting them as hopeless victims needing benevolent men's moral guidance interfered with the singers' benign voices. But other male singers have, without any moral scruples, slotted the images of women into the traditional but oppressive continuum of women as 'dangerous' and 'loose'. In the song 'Sandra' by Samson Chibvamushure and the Zig-Zag band the woman is a wandering 'prostitute' who can only be tamed by marriage:

> Sandra, there is somebody who will marry you.
> My friend if only you become submissive
> And abstain from wandering, hopping
> from one man to another

If 'Sandra' attempts to morally reclaim and rehabilitate the woman by way of marriage – itself an institution of controlling female reproductive powers – System Tazvida's 'Anodyiwa Haataure' ('One who spends on women does not tell until the moment of breaking') presents women as materialistic and outright crooks who cannot be trusted. Again, as in 'Sandra', 'Anodyiwa Haataure' gives a one-sided view of women. The song does not explore why some women have adopted 'predatory' tactics of survival which imply 'preying' on men, in post-independence Zimbabwe. But interestingly, the tendency to scapegoat women, depicting them in negative terms, is not confined to male singers only. For example, in 'Stembeni', Busi Ncube castigates the woman for leaving the children at home at night in order to frequent the beer-halls in the high-density suburbs of Harare:

> Stembeni you go to the night clubs
> leaving children alone
> Stembeni, my mother's child,
> you are cruel and wrong.

In short then, if both male and female artists show a consistent pattern in depicting women as 'dangerous' and 'loose' – terms which imply that women must be controlled and rendered powerless in both the public and private domain – there must be a master narrative to which the artists are responding and affirming. Indeed, in 1984, the nationalist government instructed its security agents (police) to round up women walking alone at night in Harare on the unfounded excuse that they were dangerous prostitutes bent on undermining the social fabric (Vambe in Pearce 1998: 11). The state's negative attitudes are partly based on traditional Shona perceptions of women as inferior and the attitudes which, during the colonial era, were transformed by capitalism which demanded submissive African women for the smooth running of capital and business. Elizabeth Schmidt notes that

> The convergent interests of African and European men thus set the stage for their collaboration in the control of African women. European gender ideology, bolstered by reinvented 'tradition' and reconstituted 'customary' law, served as the primary instruments of female control. (Schmidt 1992: 98)

It is therefore possible for artists such as Zhakata to criticise the nationalist economic policies in the same song that reinforces the traditional idea of women as men's inferior other. In other words, the degree to which individual artists, male or female, challenge and collude with the state all at once, in keeping the images of the women down, depends on the artists' social awareness which, as reflected in the songs, is itself uneven and inconsistent.

But the other sense of the term 'dangerous' in reference to female singers implies an acknowledgement of women's capacity to envision a world in which they can contest dominant negative images of womanhood in some men's minds. Thus

> through their expressive art [women] could both reshape and control in a way that was otherwise not possible. This notion of power relates to the acceptance in many African societies of licence, in some situations, within song and poetry – that singers may tell terrible things in song and poetry, set out what is not usually heard and survive with impunity. (Gunner 1994: 118).

In post-independence Zimbabwe the tradition of female singers that readily lends itself to the questioning of negative images of women in life is associated with Susan Mapfumo and, to some extent, Stella Chiweshe (ibid. 129). In 'KwaMurewa' Susan Mapfumo sings of a woman who is being abandoned by her husband for a young wife. The prophetic line 'I will end up without a home' in the song echoes Susan Mapfumo's own life which ended with illness, poverty and death. While Mapfumo's song might appear to link her voice with those of male/female artists who see women as victims, Mapfumo's later life after independence, beleaguered by squalor, underlines the difficulties facing women who want to take up music as a career. But both 'KwaMurewa' and another of Susan Mapfumo's songs, 'Baba Vabhoi' ('Father of boy'), which complains about a husband who does not bring adequate money to the family, helped to push the debate between men and women over marriage and a wife's rights into the public domain. This way, female singers such as Susan Mapfumo attempted to deconstruct the nationalist mythology of 'collective national interests' by slotting in their own voices which asserted the desire for space not only for economic fullfilment, but to 'sing' and 'inscribe' their own history and identity on the nation emerging from the contradictory processes of history.

In conclusion, the use of popular songs in post-independence Zimbabwe cannot be reduced to 'gender' essences or be assigned a 'class' belonging-ness. In the early period of the 1980s the Zimbabwean state sought to reshape and re-direct popular artists so as to make them produce meanings which the leaders agreed with. Popular singers responded in a contradictory manner often promoting the leaders' interests, even as the same singers resisted and protested against state policies which were deemed hostile to the welfare of the ordinary people. In the late 1980s and 1990s younger African singers were more strident in their criticism of the failure of government's macro-economic efforts. But even here, some young artists reinforced myths of the inferiority of women even as their songs of political protest were challenging the state's assumptions of collective national interests. Male and female singers of the 1990s who projected the image of women as 'dangerous' and 'loose' were countered by a more radical tradition of female singers associated with Susan Mapfumo who sought space for economic fullfilment as well as space to 'sing' and 'inscribe' their own voice on the history of a nation emerging from contradictory social processes of struggle. In short, the ground upon which the voices of the artists acquiesce, resist, accommodate, incorporate and challenge the views of the state and those of ordinary citizens in the country truly defines what is 'popular' in the songs. Here, something new, or a negotiated version of reality is always arrived at, only to await further transformation in new encounters and struggles.

WORKS CITED

Gunner, Liz (ed.), *Politics and Performance: Theatre, Poetry and Song in Southern Africa*, Johannesburg: University of Witwatersrand Press, 1994.

Meena, R. (ed.), *Gender in Southern Africa: Conceptual and Theoretical Issues*, Harare: SAPES Books, 1992.

Pearce, C. (ed.), *The Zimbabwean Review* Quarterly 4.3, July/September, 1998.

Pongweni, A.J.C., *Songs that won the Liberation War*, Harare: The College Press, 1982.

Samupindi, C., *Pawns*, Harare: Baobab Books, 1992.

Schmidt, E., *Peasants, Traders and Wives: Shona Women in the history of Zimbabwe*, 1870–1939, Harare: Baobab Books and London: James Currey, 1994.

Spencer-Walters, T. (ed.), *Orality, Literacy and the Fictive Imagination: African and Diasporan Literature*, Michigan: Bedford Publishers, 1999.

Storey, J. (ed.), *Cultural Theory and Popular Culture: A Reader*, London: Harvester Wheatsheaf, 1994.

de Waal, V., *The Politics of Reconciliation*, Harare: The College Press, 1992.

Wilkins, K. G. (ed.), 'Media Development', *Journal of the World Association for Christian Communication* XLII.2, 1996.

Zindi, F., *Roots Rocking in Zimbabwe*, Gweru: Mambo Press, 1985.

The Representation of Violence,
the Individual, History & the Land
in Chinodya's *Harvest of Thorns*
& Nyamfukudza's *The Non-Believer's Journey*

Jo Dandy

I This paper aims to discuss how Chinodya and Nyamfukudza represent violence in *Harvest of Thorns* (1989) and *The Non-Believer's
Journey* (1980), how the private and the public realms of consciousness
interact in the novels, and the predominance of themes of history and the
land. The motifs of the journey and of the forest are also important in both
these texts, and I will consider these images particularly in relation to the
theme of landscape. The two novels have a lot in common, not least the
land itself, as the same, recognisable territory dominates each text,
including twin journeys from the town or city to the wild and rough countryside near the border with Mozambique – the territory of the guerillas
which are central to the texts.

II T. O. McLoughlin asserts that 'Violence is both a necessity and
inevitable in most recent Zimbabwean fiction' (1984: 110). In *Harvest
of Thorns* images of violence are suppressed ones and suffering is consistently represented by the inability to speak, by silence. Even as a child,
Benjamin is silent in the face of heavy physical punishment, for instance
after his arrest following the burning of the beerhall when he is beaten by
both the police and then by his father.[1] The account of the attempted
suicide of his mother is never voiced directly, we learn of it only through
the background whisperings of Benjamin's schoolmates (96).

The silence of the guerillas, peasants and other figures caught up in the
war is at times a matter of necessity. The combatants are all given a new
identity, a war name, so that their true identities remain a secret. The
peasants are unable to speak freely about the war or the guerillas for fear
of the police and soldiers or informers. However, silence is also a symbol
of unspeakable horror and suffering in the novel, as is evident in the
depiction of the inhabitants of the guerilla camp: 'Every week the
numbers swelled. Combatants, refugees, people caught in crossfire,
fugitives whose tongues were clamped by the horror of what they had left
behind, whose muted eyes spoke of suffering' (132).[2]

After his return home, Benjamin refuses to talk about his violent experiences during the war, 'Why don't we just not talk about it, mother?' (9), and he refers to his own silence towards the end of the novel, significantly relating it to the central image of the land, 'There's nothing to talk about really. If the bush could speak then it could tell the story. When you are trying to piece together the broken fragments of your life it hurts to look back. ... What is there to talk about when people are too busy to listen and too quick to forget?' (272). Nkazana is similarly unable to speak about the violence which she has endured, 'That pregnant girl we left at home had her full supper of the war. There's not one girl in this town who has seen half of what she has. If she could speak she could tell you how the soldiers burnt out her village and how her parents were found floating in the river with their throats cut. ...' (273).[3] This image of the inability to voice violent experiences in the novel is extended through the anonymity attached to Benjamin's band of guerillas during the account of some of the most violent conflicts of the war, for example the murder of Farmer Mellecker. This scene is related from the point of view of the foreman, and deliberately does not name the combatants. It is only much later in the text during Benjamin's own reflections that we know for certain that it was his group who killed the farmer (158–65; 229). In the same way, during the story of Nkazana's rescue and the burning of her village, she remains unnamed, and is only linked to the episode by association, through Benjamin's later account of the murder of her parents to Dickson (273). There is also the whole untold story of Benjamin's family's experiences during the war which is another example of the presence of silence in the novel.[4]

Given such constant suppression and muting of images of violence by Chinodya, it is significant that some of the most expressive passages providing the deepest insights into Benjamin's suffering are portrayed through a torrent of his thoughts addressed to his mother but that she will never read or hear, written in italics and without punctuation, symbolising his lack of articulation, and set apart from the action in separate chapters, for example:

> you'll never see these words or hear them because I have no pen or paper on which to write them and not even these trees and rock can hear them ...
> I'm saying this because I have to say something sometimes because we don't talk about these things among ourselves... (148)

Thus, when Benjamin does finally speak of his experiences to Dickson at the end of the novel it is in stark contrast to his previous silence. Given this contrast, the image of Dickson at this point 'urging him on with his silence' (272) can be perceived as double-edged.

In *The Non-Believer's Journey*, however, it is paradoxically the constant act of discussing the war and its politics which is used to cover over the realities of the violence by those who do not want to become involved in the conflict. The protagonist, Sam, is terrified of the violence surrounding him, whether from the soldiers or the guerillas, and in vain tries desperately to remain detached from the realities of the war. The representation of violence is in this way closely linked to the dichotomy of the private and public, or the individual and collective in the text. In Nyamfukudza's work 'violence is seen not as the redemptive force which public rhetoric claims but as arbitrary and destructive of the individual. It is as though the process of liberation is more meaningless for the individual, particularly if he is sceptical, than the experience of oppression' (McLoughlin 1984: 113).

III Various levels of consciousness emerge through a consideration of the interaction between the private and public realms of experience in *Harvest of Thorns*. One of the more obvious forms of this structure is the enforced suppression of true identity in the guerilla camps. In this way, it is necessary for Benjamin to keep a large proportion of his own experience to himself. Consequently, the identity of Pasi Nemasellout can be seen as representative of the public sphere of his consciousness, whilst the name of Benjamin Tichafa belongs entirely to the suppressed and private. The image of these varying levels of consciousness is extended to other characters in the novel, for example the camp commander is described as having 'eyes that glazed over the details of a scene before taking it in' (121). It is only after Benjamin's total submersion in his public role as a combatant, that his childhood experiences concerning the political situation in his country can be fully comprehended, 'you knew it when you left home and left school but you didn't really know it, until this hunger and this darkness and these stars and now hearing it made the anger eat you like pepper in your nose and you wondered how you had been so blind and passive' (129). Benjamin connects the violence he encounters in the war to his own personal childhood experiences. For example, when he is forced by his colleagues to beat the peasant woman Mai Tawanda to death, he is unable to dissociate her figure from the image of his mother, and the episode is linked in his mind to the tragic accident when he crippled his brother, 'her voice was like your voice in the bedroom after we came back from the hospital when the doctor said there was nothing to do but to amputate' (217).

The fragmentation of society through the imposition of colonialism has led to a more individualised narrative consciousness in *The Non-Believer's Journey*. Nyamfukudza contemplates the position and powerlessness of the individual in a war-torn community, as he is inextricably caught up in the violence. McLoughlin identifies a major theme in Zimbabwean writing as 'the isolation of the individual from his community' (McLoughlin 1984: 116) and locates a clear example of the manifestation of this tendency in *The Non-Believer's Journey*.[5] 'The effects of colonialism and the necessity for violence so disorientate the individual that Nyamfukudza's Sam tries to preserve his individuality, however sordid, in spite of the community' (ibid.). Sam is isolated from his community, both in the city and the village, due to his lack of faith in the war. His confusion is contrasted to the communal peasant consciousness, as is noted by McLoughlin, 'Nyamfukudza suggests that the war brings out a strength in the rural people's acceptance of suffering which Sam cannot understand' (ibid.: 112). It is Sam's inability, then, to unite with his community in their struggle for liberation that is the cause of his death. He is unable to remain separate from the concerns of war: 'There is no place in this violent country for the individual who does not give himself to the communal belief that liberation is possible. Unlike Marechera, Nyamfukudza makes his controlling consciousness answerable to the socio-political context of the narrative' (ibid.). Thus, *The Non-Believer's Journey* is a story of the incapacity of the individual to define his own space in a society dominated by war, or to survive and to escape the responsibility of the collective.

IV Both novels reveal a deep preoccupation with history. In *Harvest of Thorns* Chinodya examines different and conflicting ways of writing and telling history, or as Elizabeth Tonkin has put it, different 'representations of pastness' (1994: 27). For instance, the whole of Chapter 26 is written in the form of varying accounts by the villagers of the battle on the hill:

> Now many stories have been told about that battle on the hill in Sachikonye's village. Many many stories, some true, some not so true, some highly coloured by the terror and imagination of the people who heard about what happened from those who saw it happen ...
> It is said by some that ...
> And some stories have it that ...
> Some of the little children who were there say ...
> And many tongues have it that ... (212–14)

Chinodya narrates the history of the nation's colonisation as an oral historical account, in the story told by the guerilla leader Baas Die to the villagers (171–81). In the customary African mode of telling history, the story is rooted in local tradition. It also bases the conflict firmly on the white man's expropriation of the land.

Like Chinodya, Nyamfukudza is concerned with differing versions of facts in his novel,[6] referring, for instance, to discrepancies between the casualty figures cited by the guerillas and by the government.[7] However, history, in its traditional local form, is also portrayed as a uniting force in the face of the violence of war in *The Non-Believer's Journey*: 'If there was a time when people needed their traditions, their sense of identity and their past, it is now. I don't go to church, because I don't go along with

picking up a belief because some missionary white man says mine is bad
and his is better, especially now when I am fighting the white man!' (91).
Significantly, this extract is voiced by Mudomeni, a figure much older
and wiser than Sam, who is unable to align himself completely with the
freedom fighters and asserts that 'You can't take everything from the past
wholesale' (92).

History, for Nyamfukudza, is essentially linked to the land, because of
both the traditional dependency of the local people on the land and their
dispossession by the colonisers. Thus the footpath, carved by a multitude
of villagers' feet over many years becomes, in stark contrast to the tarmac
road of the white man which takes a longer route, a mark of the people's
history, in perfect harmony with the land itself:

> Does anyone ever make a deliberate choice as to the exact route of a footpath, he
> wondered, or does it follow the line of least resistance, where the trees or grass
> are thinner, bearing generally in the desired direction like rainwater finding its
> way to the sea? Someone, however, must one day have walked it first, enabling
> the next man to see the trodden grass and know that one like him had wandered
> thereon before. So we take comfort, he thought, in following in our fellow man's
> footsteps. (30)

The image of the land is powerful throughout both novels. It is closely
associated with local history, and above all with the war. 'The Zimbabwean *chimurenga* was a guerilla war and it was in important ways a
people's war, with land and a sense of dispossession at its centre' (Gunner
1991: 77). The landscape of the built-up areas is sharply contrasted with
the wilds of the countryside in each text, and the journey of the protagonist from city to country is a central (and parallel) image in both. The
image of the township in *Harvest of Thorns* is a crowded and squalid
one, for example: 'Everywhere there were mountains of brick and sand
on the side of the roads. Some of the houses had been finished – these
had a sprawling, squashed look even where the extensions were newly
painted' (77).

A clear distinction emerges between the busy, crowded, stifling surroundings of the township, and the freedom and expansiveness of the
open country. 'The bus hurtled out of the smoky atmosphere of the
township and the sky became clear as they drove through a patch of
forest' (7). As a guerilla, Benjamin (or Pasi) returns to his cultural roots
and becomes a part of the land itself, reliant on its protection, such as for
food or camouflage, for example, 'I don't feel now I belong to anything
other than this soil on which I sleep' (148) and 'The forest had reclaimed
him – outcast from the huts and houses where humans dwelt – to its
kingdom of leaf and claw' (229). He is continually described in terms of
the landscape, 'Benjamin scurried like a leaf in the wind' (118).

The land also represents traditional values and beliefs, and the spirit
medium, the *svikiro*, is a symbol of this bond between landscape and spirituality in both *Harvest of Thorns* and *The Non-Believer's Journey*. She is

the figure to whom the villagers turn for advice, and when she speaks she voices the feelings of the earth itself, 'The soil is not happy and the skies are frowning' (247). Personification of the landscape is used by Chinodya to symbolise the strength of the relationship between the people and the land. One of the most striking examples of this technique is the comparison of the marks left on the land by the war with human wounds or scars: 'Amazing, he thought, that certain areas could completely heal, while some festered like stubborn wounds and others, like the suburbs on the hill, chose to remain untouched by war. He looked at the faces of sparkling glass, pinewood, stone' (7). Other examples of the personification of landscape and of the inanimate objects of the township are plentiful, 'TV aerials perched on the roofs' (6), 'they huddled in that womb' [with reference to the underground tunnel at the guerilla camp] (121) and 'The township houses crouch darkly in fatigued rows ... The battered Renault ... shudders along mirrored pavements ... and coughs up suburban curves. The hospital leaps out of the grove' (275).

One of the most significant uses of land imagery in *Harvest of Thorns*, however, is in the description of the baby boy born to Benjamin and Nkazana at the end of the novel, a symbol of the simultaneous rebirth of the nation. Just as the nation has been renamed Zimbabwe, an African name as opposed to Rhodesia, the child is named Zvenyika,[8] an African name as opposed to the names of the previous generation – Esther, Benjamin and Peter. The parallels between the new-born child and the new nation are enhanced by the images of the landscape which are used to portray the child's features – he has 'a little hill of a nose ... [and] two brown leaves of ears' (276).

Nyamfukudza uses imagery of the landscape to an even greater extent in *The Non-Believer's Journey*. Again, a strong contrast is set up between the built-up areas and the country. The very noise and bustle of the city is used as an image of suffering by Nyamfukudza, 'After a couple of minutes listening to the hum from the built up area which rose and fell, sometimes faint, then gradually swelling to a continuous moan, he suddenly felt depressed. The sound carried to him the image of weeping, sorrowing hordes of men and women' (6). The land is tied to the people's sense of identity and community in the novel, so that, when Sam speaks of their dispossession of the land, he says 'They had been robbed of something valuable, something which had made them feel a spark of togetherness' (24). The city is associated with slavery to the white man in *The Non-Believer's Journey*, whilst the countryside is an image of freedom and embodies the struggle, inevitably bound to the image of the freedom fighters living and fighting in the wilds of the mountainous territory on the border with Mozambique, as in *Harvest of Thorns*.[9] Thus, when Sam travels from the city to the country, it is seen as an escape, 'In no time at all they were free of buildings and out in the open where mile after mile of green maizefields spread out on either side of the road as far as the eye could see' (25). The country where they are headed, however, is wild and untamed. It is this country that is associated fully with the guerillas and the promise of freedom, 'It was ironic, he thought, that this same wild and difficult country into which they had been hustled was proving to be the biggest ally of the men fighting to bring down the government' (27).

The guerillas themselves are depicted with images of the forest, an image often used in African literature, but reworked in this text, and extended for example to include images of camouflage and bush warfare. Sam dissociates the image of the forest in his own mind from the context of traditional fears of 'mysterious spirits of ancestors' (97), and transfers this inherited fear of the forest on to his fear of the guerillas, whom he describes as 'men just like himself who suddenly wandered into the middle of the villages as if out of nowhere, with guns strapped onto their backs, bringing the forest right into their homes' (97). The image of the forest is also used as a parallel to Sam's confusion about the war. At one point Sam is lost in the forest and is desperately trying to find a way out. As the forest is representative of the struggle for independence in the novel, this image is indicative of Sam's struggle to find a way of dealing with the war. He is unable to escape from the forest, just as he is unable to escape from the war. He is constantly attempting to maintain a position apart from the conflict, but in the end he cannot escape and is forced into making a choice, 'if he could get out, find a way out of the forest. The trees seemed to hem him in from every direction' (99).

Like Chinodya, Nyamfukudza personifies the landscape as an image of the bond between the people and the land. Of the Kachuru mountain he says: 'As he gazed at it, it somehow evoked thoughts and images of a guardian monster, massive and silent, crouching patiently, biding its time' (84). In addition he refers to caves and tunnels 'within its belly' (84). Other examples of the personification of the land and the elements in this text are: 'two conical hills which pointed up like a pair of ripe young breasts' (70), 'in the night the dark was moving in with all its allies to strangle him' (72) or 'a few scattered stars winking here and there, as if reluctantly' (104). Subsequently, the land is used to depict images of the war or the people's suffering in the novel. For example the sky is described as having streaks of 'blood-red' in it (86). Sam feels a dangerous force around him as he walks through the country after the curfew, and almost expects this hidden danger to manifest itself physically in his surroundings, 'Some tangible proof of the danger and violence lurking around him would have helped to settle his feelings one way or another. If there had been, for instance, the faintest rumbling of thunder in the hills ahead, he thought half seriously, something to show that the early evening quiet was a deceptive fraud' (69). Sam feels, then, that the land itself possesses a force to be reckoned with, 'It had been the strangest of feelings, that this rugged piece of ground over which he had run and herded cattle throughout his childhood now held a force which would wrestle with, and probably succeed in altering the course and future of, the country' (97).

The landscape is intrinsically linked to history by Nyamfukudza. The following extract contemplates not only the extent to which the history and traditions of the local people are embedded within the land, but also the richness of the land itself as a resource and its seizure by the white colonisers, and in addition reveals a concern with naming:

> Had it not been for the war, the hill to his left would by now have been blasted apart to sink a mine for the rich vein of iron which rose to the surface at that point. The people in the neighbouring villages had already been told they would have to move off. What a queer sight it would have been, he thought, after so long, grafted into the legends and memories of the local people, for one of the hills to be left without a partner. The name, Chimhanda, forked members, would have become intriguingly meaningless, abandoned by what it was called into being to identify. (70)

Like history, the land is also an important source of unity in both texts. As a focal point of the struggle, the desire to reclaim the land provided a common objective between the guerillas and politicians in Zimbabwe, who are portrayed, particularly by Nyamfukudza, as existing in a state of great disharmony. As Terence Ranger notes: 'This intense focus on the recovery of lost lands was given every encouragement not only by guerilla political education but also by the campaigning speeches of the ZANU/PF candidates in the 1980 elections.' (1985: 287).

VI   The motif of the journey has been used widely in African literature, and is a dominant image in both texts under discussion here:

> In her discussion of the journey motif in African literature, Mortimer points to the journey as a theme shared by both coloniser and colonised. She proposes three reasons for its prominence; first, the significance of the journey in oral literature, second, the importance of the journey in the European novel, finally the mobility of African peoples ... postcolonial writers take up imperial motifs, of which the journey is a prominent example, and re-use them ... the journey motif has an African as well as an imperial provenance and an ongoing significance. (Brogden 1994: 3)

The journey motif is reworked in this way in both *Harvest of Thorns* and *The Non-Believer's Journey*. For example, as acknowledged by McLoughlin, the journey can be seen as a metaphor for the war itself.[10] It can also be seen as 'indicative of spiritual alienation' (McLoughlin 1984: 110) in the texts. The image of the journey is developed to a fuller extent in *The Non-Believer's Journey*, recalling Mikhail Bakhtin's notion of the road through time and space, 'the spatial and temporal paths of the most varied people intersect at one spatial and temporal point.... Time, as it were, fuses together with space and flows in it; this is the source of the rich metaphorical expansion of the image of the road as a course' (Bakhtin

1981: 245). In this context, Nyamfukudza's image of the people on the bus journey as being dissociated from time and place takes on a new relevance. Sam observes in his reminiscing over previous bus journeys when he was much more able to associate with the people around him, that 'It was as if he and all those around him had been insidiously dissociated from the realities of time and place, and the multi-rhythmic pulsations of the traditional tunes were the throbbings of their hearts beating in unison in some land far removed from a hampering, shackled life under the white man's rule in the city' (24).

VII In summary, both *Harvest of Thorns* and *The Non-Believer's Journey* are texts rich in information about the Zimbabwean land and people against the violent backdrop of the Independence War. Interesting parallels can be drawn between Chinodya's and Nyamfukudza's work in the context of African literature as a whole, most especially in the exploration of the complex reworking of the motifs of the journey and the forest. However, the most remarkable aspect of these works, and the most striking parallel between the two, is the image of the land itself, the immensity of its physical domination in the texts, and its ability to simultaneously represent the past and future of a nation.

NOTES

1. Chinodya 1989: 86–90. All subsequent references to this edition will be referred to by page numbers in brackets.
2. The silent confrontation of violence by the guerillas is linked to their youth by a villager, 'what young men not to cry or flinch or show signs of pain, what young men to bear the weight of death on their own' (16).
3   Yet another example of the inability of the characters to voice their experiences during the war can be seen on pp. 271–2, when Dickson says: 'A cousin of mine was in the bush for five years. He's a captain in the army now. When he came back he wouldn't say a word about his experiences. He wouldn't be drawn out at all.'
4. Benjamin's parents seem to change greatly during his absence and most notably they separate in this period, yet this part of the story is left untold by Chinodya.
5. 'Novels and short stories since 1975 have regarded the inner life of the individual as drawn inevitably to violent protest against the colonial system.' (McLoughlin 1984:110).
6. Despite this interrogation, the novel is full of 'factual' information concerning the political situation (eg. land rights), much more so than *Harvest of Thorns*.
7. Nyamfukudza 1980: 30. All subsequent references to this edition will be referred to by page numbers in brackets.
8. It is interesting in this context to note the meaning of the name Zvenyika which is 'of the nation' 'of politics' or 'of the land'.
9. Although the contrast between city and countryside is used as an image of captivity and freedom in both texts, the image of the forest, given its wide-ranging implications and usages in African (and European) literature, is not monolithic – thus the forest represents fear as well as hope, danger as well as protection.
10. McLoughlin refers to 'the war – variously imaged as a bush fire, a wife, a journey' with reference to Zimbabwean poetry about the war (114).

WORKS CITED

Bakhtin, M.M., *The Dialogic Imagination*, Austin: University of Texas Press, 1981.

Brogden, Mark, 'Migrancy and the Journey in Four West African Texts: Ama Ata Aidoo – *Our Sister Killjoy*; Cheikh Hamidou Kane – *Ambiguous Adventure*; Ahmadou Kourouma – *The Suns of Independence*; Camara Laye – *The Radiance of the King*, University of London, SOAS, MA dissertation, 1994.

Chinodya, Shimmer, *Harvest of Thorns*, Harare: Baobab Books, 1989.

Gunner, Liz, 'Power, Popular Consciousness and the Fictions of War: Hove's *Bones* and Chinodya's *Harvest of Thorns*', *African Languages and Cultures*, 4.1, 1991.

McLoughlin, T.O., 'Black Writing in English from Zimbabwe' in G.D. Killam (ed.) *The Writing of East and Central Africa*, London: Heinemann, 1984.

Nyamfukudza, S., *The Non-Believer's Journey*, London: Heinemann, 1980.

Ranger, Terence, *Peasant Consciousness and Guerilla War in Zimbabwe*, London: James Currey, 1985.

Tonkin, Elizabeth, 'History and the Myth of Realism', in Raphael Samuel and Paul Thompson, *The Myths We Live By*, London: Routledge, 1994.

'Speaking Crystals:
The Poetry of Lionel Abrahams
& South African Liberalism

Dan Wylie

> Our territory is inhabited by a number of races speaking different languages
> and living on different historical levels. A few groups still live as they did in
> prehistoric times. Others ... who were displaced by successive invasions, exist
> on the outer margins of history ... [A] variety of epochs live side by side in the
> same areas or a very few miles apart, ignoring or devouring each other.[1]

Octavio Paz's description of his native Mexico could as easily be of South
Africa – even the 'New', post-liberation South Africa. Varieties of intract-
able otherness remain entrenched in group mentalities, cutting across
politically fraught efforts to create a 'national culture', and complicating
the flattening effects of global media cultures. Racial categorisations and
epithets continue to fly despite the official dismantling of apartheid. In
an embattled middle ground between traditionally leftwing, often violent
activism, and equally violent, rightwing apartheid, South African liberal-
humanist thinkers, politicians and writers have habitually found themselves (some would say satisfyingly) attacked from both sides. The recent
poetry of Lionel Abrahams focuses particularly keenly the ways in which
the political contestations articulate with the aesthetics of literary production in South Africa.

As I was completing this paper in June 1999, South Africa was undergoing its second democratic election. The liberals' Democratic Party made
strong gains in votes, but scarcely enough to assuage its customary noisy
marginalisation. The strongly racial bias of the voting patterns reinforces
a long-standing perception that liberalism entails little more than a
defence of white suburban privilege. The DP's so-called 'muscular liberalism' has widely been condemned as a drift to the 'white right'. Contra-
dictorily, ANC minister Kader Asmal, writing just three days before the
election, condemned the DP for having abandoned 'a better self', the
liberalism of Joseph Raz and John Rawls, in favour of 'the libertarian
excesses and self-servingness of Thatcherism and Robert Nozick'.[2] The
split here is roughly between those (liberals and non-liberals alike) who
would characterise liberalism as a coherent, absolutist ideology (there can
be no 'unconscious liberalism' as Antony Holiday puts it), and those who

tend towards a liberalism more mindful of contingency and historicity, a 'triumph of experience over dogma'.[3]

Party-based, sectarian rhetorics, though numbingly boring, have had their impact on debates concerning the role of poetry. A crude, racially-inflected antithesis has repeatedly opposed a 'liberal-humanist' aesthetic of lyrically contemplative, cerebral individualism with an activist rhetoric of urgent public commitment. Black poets expressed the problem even before apartheid: this is H. I.E. Dhlomo in the 1940s:

> Why do I sap my powers in singing songs
> Of Nature's beauty or of untroubled bloodless things,
> When I should break like thunder on the wrongs
> That bind humanity in chains of maddening things?
> Full now I realise there is no beauty
> Save beauty of a free and healthy, happy
> Union of men and women[4]

The equation of 'beauty' with cocooned white privilege is both understandable and untenable. The racist label is unfair to the extent that the aesthetic antithesis of contemplation and activism has affected all societies in turmoil, regardless of race; there are deeper patterns of human association at work. The stereotypes of the aloof lyricist and the self-sublimating fighter are tropes historically entrenched in Western political and literary thought (to which even the liberation movements are massively indebted). The activists' demand that poetry actually make something happen, or at the very least unproblematically reflect one ideologically predetermined realm of 'reality' – the plight of the racially oppressed – is a linguistically impossible dream, and involves an assumption that certain kinds of social advance are necessarily more important than others. And who is to determine that the longterm, subtle evolution of the contemplative self, say, will not prove more historically important than any immediate change of government or racial policy, however necessary the latter may be?

Further complicating the issue is that many of the most vicious attacks on liberal-humanist poetry have come from other whites (often poets themselves) – and many of those from within the academic institutions which these same complainants characterise as liberal-humanist bastions. Rory Ryan in 1990 delivered a scathing attack on what he called the 'humanist-colonial ... tradition'.

> One of the most seriously hegemonic and repressive gestures produced by humanism has been to offer up its social-cultural goals as 'truth', and its methods (of self-perpetuation and glorification) as 'truth-seeking'.[5]

Echoing Asmal, Ryan does allow the existence and value of an ideal humanist programme: 'At its best, humanism has always stuttered and faltered; at its worst, it is smoothly confident and self-righteous'.[6] The ability of the humanist institution to tolerate and assimilate antithetical views (including his own, he confesses) is, Ryan concludes, only another ploy for preserving itself, rather than a sign of intellectual robustness.

Abrahams expressed dismay at Ryan's 'tone of paranoid omniscience' and he thought the 'charge of sustained hegemonic conspiracy' absurd.[7] This is an opinion refracted through Abrahams' insistence on the primacy of the individual viewpoint. His poetry shows that his conventional humanistic appeal to 'imagination, delight, beauty', as opposed to a view of literature as 'an arcane type of socio-political instrumentality', is self-aware in a rigorously individualistic way. Since what constitutes imaginative power, what delights, what's judged beautiful, are inevitably culturally constructed or inflected, Abrahams can't quite escape the charges of being locked in a bourgeois 'language cell'[8] of suburban privilege. But as he has averred elsewhere, '*Once one has dealt with the requirements of survival*, one's responsibility is to grace life with adventure, poetry and humour'.[9] The poetries devoted to survival and beauty, he implies, may pragmatically exclude one another in certain circumstances, but the two need not deny one another's validity.

The dispiriting controversies over the role of the lyrical poet are vacuous in the sense that both activists and liberal-humanists have argued on the basis of implicit notions of some or other absolute truth, and on the assumption that those truths can be made self-evident through rational argument or empirical observation. As Mark Johnson has persuasively argued, however,[10] this underpinning notion of rational truth is itself not capable of complete proof or demonstration; the implicit absolute moral holism on which it depends is fundamentally metaphorical in nature. At crucial junctures, Abrahams' poetry exposes the metaphoric structure of this moral being in a spirit which is neither absolutist nor purely relativistic, but is pragmatically self-stabilising around what Johnson calls a Kantian 'image of a community of free and equal beings who are able to think and act for themselves in a manner that respects the right of other people to do the same'.[11] What is important here is that it is an *image*: any such moral community depends, in short, on an act of the imagination. Still, the crudities of oppositional thought are the political realities of South African life, and some poems in Abrahams' 1995 volume, *A dead tree full of live birds*,[12] evidence sharp anxieties about those oppositions. The best poems, I think, offer one path through the labyrinth of ideological reassessments now in train – one which more poets now are seeing as a possibility freshly freed from 'liberal guilt'.

I think I am right in saying that no other South African writer has been honoured with a *Reader* on his sixtieth birthday, and a creative kind of *festschrift*, compiled by many of the writers who owe inspirational debt to Abrahams, on his seventieth. In the latter volume, *A Writer in Stone*, his editors characterise him as (in the words of one of his own poems) the 'relationship man', who has fostered the careers of dozens of writers over fifty years, and introduced to the world such local luminaries as Oswald

Mtshali, Mongane Wally Serote, Ruth Miller and Herman Charles Bosman.[13] Few people have had such an impact on the literature of this country – almost certainly to the detriment of his own output, which remains one 'novel in 18 stories', *The Celibacy of Felix Greenspan*, four collections of poetry, and a swathe of articles and other trenchant interventions in the literary controversies of his time.

Abrahams' views on his own liberalism have been as controversial as any. Patrick Cullinan summarises:

> Though his standpoint is unequivocally 'liberal' it is ... a very tough liberalism which sees doubt as a creative and active force and which makes no apology for spurning fashionable ideologies of the left or the complacent brutalities of the right.[14]

It is perhaps oversimplifying to say 'unequivocally'. Abrahams might have acknowledged himself openly 'liberal' at one time, adopting it, characteristically, because liberalism 'was getting a bad name for behaviours I approved of'[15] – behaviours like those of the Magistrate in J M Coetzee's great novel, *Waiting for the Barbarians*, of which character Abrahams wrote warmly: 'this soft man – this humanitarian, this pacifist, this agnostic, this lecher of justice, this (ah, yes!) liberal'.[16] This has mutated into scorn for all such ideological labels:

> I don't like labels. It's a question of what I like and what I don't like. I prefer acting individually. I dislike organisational discipline. I distrust activism.... I distrust most kinds of idealism, especially social – impersonal – idealism. I distrust intensified morality.[17]

If this resort to the imponderables of taste begs the question of what social forces, chosen precursors, and preferred reading has 'constructed' that taste, Abrahams' answer is, on one level, clear enough: having found himself at one time 'besieged by ideologies', and protecting himself with what he terms a 'fastidious dissociation', he has adopted a more thoroughgoing individualism:

> I no longer fear to embrace or be embraced by an ideology. I no longer hover in confusion, struggling to discover on which side the truth lies. As far as ideologists are concerned, perhaps, by ceasing to be either an agnostic or an enemy or a fugitive, I have become more of a lost case than ever. I have become now, not a dilettante of ideologies, since ideologies do not delight me, but an eclectic.[18]

In the apartheid context, it has always been easy to characterise this absorption in one's own lostness as itself a luxury of liberalist leisure, and some of Abrahams' poems evince a continuing anxiety over the question. For instance, a certain tendency to caricature the violence of activism surfaces in the title poem to *A dead tree full of live birds*, in the stark figure of 'another' revolutionary 'youth,/ his bunched up fist aloft', who declaims, '"I am Azania ... I have no time for liberals..."' The hand-me-down, gauchely sectarian sign of the raised fist is, Abrahams implies, part of the poverty of rhetoric associated with the authoritarian 'demands of History, revolution, sociological times'[19] – the triumph of dogma over experience. Abrahams envisages a dismaying surrender of coherent thought to the 'masses':

> Poems? Dare we enjoy such shapes?
> Professors of today,
> earnestmen of justice, priests who invoke
> the holy mass of masses say:
> 'The mass extruded from the choiceless mass
> whose struggle is meaning
> suffices for the weight of art.
> The rest is custom, artifice and privilege,
> pacts between the blindly self-elect
> elect what they'll call excellent.'[20]

Abrahams portrays here a view which wishes to subsume all within its own rationalisation, to destroy or banish as frivolous the dissenting voice. As he scathingly – perhaps over-simplistically – observes elsewhere: 'Whoever speaks of "classes" and "masses" is an enemy of mankind'.[21] Against the rejection of the individually chosen and willed, the characterisation of his own considered position as mere 'artifice' and 'privilege', Abrahams wants to establish a different, but not easily achieved or expressed, set of values. 'The one sacrilege,' he writes in 'Entries Under Religion', is 'frozen purity'.[22] If any individual's history were 'Complete and permanent', it would, like Blake's Urizen, 'fill/its own eternity/ enclosed, sealed, separate'[23] – would become, in one sense, ideological 'History'. Instead, Abrahams draws inspiration, energy, and authenticity from the very fragmentariness attendant on that doubting marginalisation:

> The snapped, permitted piece
> participates in the
> continuum, the self
> unended in the whole of
> numberless otherness.[24]

The equivocation on 'unended' marks a different kind of metonymy from that expressed by the revolutionary subsumed in his cause: 'I *am* Azania.' Abrahams imagines himself a 'piece', at once painfully removed from the whole, 'snapped' off, but 'permitted' rather than condemned, participating not through a self neither irrevocably removed from society nor lost within it, but one connected to its multiplicity of 'others' through persistent acts of the imagination. (Who, however, is doing this 'permitting'? Here an anxiety over the distribution of power lurks.) For Abrahams, 'Mortality's injury is healed/ by just that brokenness'.[25] The paradox is amplified by a marvellously unsettling equivocation: the suggestion that mortality might itself *be* the injury. With its characteristic turn towards a highly individual metaphysic, the image is also the poetic expression of that self-criticism Abrahams sees as central to the humanist stance: 'if one has the luck often enough to be appalled by oneself, this is the crucible that burns one into clarity'.[26] The stubborn rigour with which that doubting brokenness is defended as valuable may itself be mentally tortuous: 'The Debater' wakes in the small hours almost frightened at his 'own didactic,/indignant voice bellowing/heartless ignorance'. This echoes, even internalises, his own critics' accusations of high-handed intolerance. Abrahams' own reply is a longing for 'the softness of shame/ the patient stillness of doubt'.[27] This is perhaps more an ideal than a state of mind actually enacted in the poems: their argumentative, impassioned structure evinces rather the mind of an irrepressible 'quarreller'.[28]

Abrahams, then, tends to express his values in terms primarily relational:

> I respond to passion but with it I require balance and courage and modesty as well. I admire cleverness, but scarcely in the absence of other qualities – warmth, humour and, again, modesty. I want boldness and originality, but coupled with considerateness. A tremulous sensitivity can be most wonderful, an enrichment, a transmutation of the fugitive moments of ordinariness – but it is worthless, a precious solipsistic pose, if it goes unaccompanied by considerateness, modesty, or humour.[29]

Although he once disparaged the pre-eminence of any 'doctrine' of style which produced only 'trivial, irresponsible and futile results', Abrahams also recognised that style was inseparable from 'the subtle wholeness of the meaning'. Perhaps too aware of the vagaries of taste to pin himself to specifics, he does say he values 'subtlety, complexity, disinterested verisimilitude, individual imaginativeness', these also being 'a matter of word music, syntactical rhythms, rich and idiosyncratic vocabulary, a distillation of the writer's unique personality, his truth, his passion'.[30] Conversely, he disparages 'obscurity, incoherence, mere soul-outpouring, self enclosure, under-craftedness, banality, blatant politicking, or sheer excess'.[31] His own poems demonstrate these tenets: never stuffy, often embodying a sustained and careful argument, using a wide but unpretentious vocabulary. In 'On Reading Berryman's Last Collection', Abrahams clearly identifies with poor John Berryman who, 'shamed and wrung beyond applause and peace/ and very breath', wrestles out of his 'extreme necessity' 'speaking crystals, honed balanced/arrowheads of praise and protest,/ poems'.[32] The measured intensities of craftsmanship implied here are the methods by which Abrahams both asserts his 'face in [his] place'[33] and rescues his deliberate vulnerability from maudlin self-pity.

Some of the imagery of 'Berryman's Last Collection' recurs in 'Flesh'. I cannot read this superb poem without a consciousness of Abrahams' almost lifelong confinement to a wheelchair by a form of palsy, Jewish Tortion Dystonia, which makes the movement of a hand, even the enunciation of a word, an enormous effort. Some lines in 'Flesh' might read as hyperbolic without this knowledge, but the poem is otherwise bare of sentimentality, it is a characteristic blend of the impassioned and the cerebral, visceral metaphor balanced against considered, almost sardonic argument. The poem grapples with the meaning of 'struggle' – a word simultaneously loaded with revolutionary overtones and in danger of irrecoverable debasement:

> Busy in my skin in my house, I receive
> rumours and news. Again and again I hear
> about too much death, too much pain,
> too much emptiness, the culpabilities,
> relentless causes and terrible ends.[34]

That first line enacts the layerings of white suburban isolation of which poets like Abrahams are so often accused, but what he hears, albeit 'mufffled, distorted,/diminished', is terrifying in its very generality, apprehended rationalistically but in cadences of biblical force. Abrahams is well aware that his busyness, however active by his own lights, is easily interpreted as frippery by those who are actually suffering that pain and emptiness; he can attend only with 'half an ear or heart'; in that perspective, his activity takes 'the form of distraction'.

After these generalities, the poem takes a dramatically personal, existential turn. Despite the suburban cocoon, he is *not* safe in his skin: his very house contains 'sufficient travail,/ the floor lies ready to bruise me,/ beat out my breath'. Even the essentials – health, safety and time to work – 'are not vouchsafed':

> I must carve them out of each slippery,
> hard-textured day, must grapple
> with the knotted minutes for those luxuries:
> my bare subsistence, a glint of meaning.[35]

There's a trace of the sardonic in classifying these as 'luxuries': it is his ideological opponents' word, rather than his. In fact he is, he seems to be saying, no less threatened by existential annihilation than those for whom the other, political 'struggle' is being waged. A meaningful existence, as the involuted metaphors enact, is not easier for him to extract: only the surrounds are different. Those metaphors are, I think, the aesthetic articulation of the imaginative morality of which Mark Johnson writes. They incorporate a notion of unremitting hard craft in a world immune to absolutes, at once impenetrable, elusive, labyrinthine and short-lived. They express the final moral reality of the limited, limiting body beneath the veneers of the idealistic and the rational. While Abrahams consistently valorises the rational, he has also warned – as did 'Blake, Keats, Nietzsche, Freud, Jung, Rudolph Steiner [and] Lawrence' – of the 'insufficiency of mind'.[36] The metaphors of bodily materiality suggest, then, that the creation of meaning itself is metaphoric, an act of the imagination. The final lines make their argumentative conclusion almost sarcastically, not, I think, dismissing the wider, 'practical' struggle, but protesting the dismissal of his own:

> This is why, for all I have heard,
> I remain, you could say, aloof,
> in practical terms, you could say,
> ignorant of the struggle.[37]

'Aloof', again, is the outsider's word, used almost mockingly – and almost self-mockingly. In this ambivalent absorption of the vocabulary of the 'Other', Abrahams expresses an imaginative act of understanding which neither rests content with, nor obliterates his sense of a valued self. So the 'aloofness' is rather a celebration of elusiveness, an assertion that the values to which Abrahams appeals are too easily dismissed as obscurantist, vague, and elitist, just because they are irreducibly strange, 'too subtle, various and individual to be amenable to revolutionary discipline'.[38] And in the stylistic foregrounding of metaphor, Abrahams inscribes the truism that the Other understood is really an Other imagined, an Other within.

Nothing is more elusive and problematic, perhaps, than Abrahams' baseline appeal to 'Human Nature', a conception he finds 'a useful, indeed indispensable, hypothesis: there are general, unique and significant qualities or capacities that bind all the members of the *homo sapiens* into a continuum'.[39] He addresses the issue in 'A Weary Creed', in which he portrays a fellow poet castigating him for clinging to this allegedly outmoded notion. Abrahams makes it clear that this 'ineluctable desideratum,/ elusive common denominator,/ everyman's grail', is not confined to some wishy-washy attachment to beauty or gentility: it is a 'putative essence/ that bleeds alike through caveman and Gautama,/ Jane Austen, Makana and Al Capone'. Though that list implies an awareness of the historical, transcultural extremes of human types, from the preliterate to the super-literary, from the spiritual master to the irredeemably evil gangster, there remains a distinctive idealism behind it, a view of society Aristotelian rather than terrifyingly Hobbesian. Like other holistic notions with moral import, this ideal of 'humanity' is necessarily an imaginative, imagined entity or commonness, a 'conceit' which 'resists description and proof,/ obstinately remains mere rhetoric'. The quality of rhetoric used in expressing this 'humanness', then, is itself the heart of the matter, and has to express its own uniqueness even as it speaks into the continuum of experience. 'A Weary Creed' concludes with just such a metaphorically heightened, brilliantly *embodied*, 'speaking crystal': one's beliefs may be ultimately inexpressible and timebound, and otherness may be ineradicable,

> Yet an ichor runs in the beating vein
> which grafts my rotting, solipsistic speck
> alive onto the pulse of history;
> and my lungs in their exclusive cell suck in
> the shared prophetic breath of speech.[40]

NOTES

1. Octavio Paz, *The Labyrinth of Solitude* (Harmondsworth: Penguin, 1990), 11. I am indebted to Don Maclennan for comment on a draft of this article.
2. 'Is Liberalism Dead or Alive?', *Sunday Times*, 30 May 1999, 23.
3. James Leatt, Theo Kneifel and Klaus Nurnberger, eds, *Contending Ideologies in South Africa* (Cape Town: David Philip, 1986), 53. For further discussion, see also Anthony Holiday, 'The truth about liberals and racists', *Mail & Guardian*, 4–10 December 1998, 25; Jeffrey Butler, Richard Elphick and David Welsh, eds. *Democratic Liberalism in South Africa: Its History and Prospect* (Cape Town: David Philip, 1987); Libby Husemayer, ed. *Watchdogs or Hypocrites?: The amazing debate on South African liberals and liberalism* (Johannesburg: Friedrich-Naumann-Stiftung, 1997).
4. 'Renunciation', in Michael Chapman, ed. *The Paperbook of South African English Poetry* (Parklands: Ad. Donker, 1986) 103.
5. Ryan, Rory, 'Literary-Intellectual Behaviour in South Africa', in Martin Trump, ed. *Rendering Things Visible: Essays on South African Literary Culture* (Johannesburg: Ravan, 1990) 2.
6. Ryan 11.
7. *South African Literary Review*, 1/2, April 1991, 16.
8. SALR, 2/4, December 1992, 12.
9. SALR 1/4, December 1991, 9 (my emphasis).
10. Mark Johnson, *Moral Imagination: Implications of Cognitive Science for Ethics* (Chicago: Chicago University Press, 1993).
11. Johnson 65–6.
12. Lionel Abrahams, *A dead tree full of live birds* (Cape Town: Snailpress, 1995).
13. Graeme Friedman and Roy Blumenthal, eds. *A Writer in Stone* (Cape Town: David Philip, 1998).
14. Patrick Cullinan, ed. *Lionel Abrahams: A Reader* (Craighall: Ad Donker, 1988), 11.
15. *Writer in Stone* 241.
16. *Reader* 264.
17. *Writer in Stone* 243.
18. *Reader* 308.
19. 'A dead tree full of live birds', *A dead tree*, 7.
20. 'On Reading Berryman's Last Poems', *A dead tree*, 18.
21. *SALR* 1/4, 8.
22. *A dead tree* 53.
23. *A dead tree* 54.
24. *A dead tree* 54.
25. *A dead tree* 54.
26. *SALR* 1/4, 8.
27. 'The Debater Wakes in the Small Hours', *A dead tree*, 52.
28. *SALR* 2/2, 8.
29. *Reader* 310.
30. *Reader* 306–8.
31. *New Coin* 34/1, June 1998, 95.
32. *A dead tree* 18.
33. *Reader* 306–7.
34. 'Flesh', *A dead tree* 14.
35. *A dead tree* 14.
36. *New Contrast* 89, March 1995, 68.
37. 'Flesh', *A dead tree* 14.
38. From an open letter to the activist poet Jeremy Cronin; *SALR* 2/2, June 1992, 8 .
39. *SALR* 2/2, 8.
40. 'A Weary Creed', *A dead tree* 15.

Personality & Self Re-Creation in Bessie Head's Art

Sophia Obiajulu Ogwude

I Since Sigmund Freud first delineated the body of knowledge known as psychoanalysis in the nineteenth century, psychoanalytic criticism has fulfilled different critical functions in literature. Fortunately, the earlier and often disconcerting studies which usually tilted towards the revelation of oedipal material and the search for sexual symbols have in more recent times been replaced by diverse critical approaches. Biographical criticism and character analysis occupy central positions in psychoanalytic studies. Although the attitude toward such analyses is frequently a distinguishing feature between various critical theories, the contention that a character takes on for the author as well as for the reader an independent personality can hardly be faulted.[1] A character is a product of life and art, and so the rationale for studying it both formally and psychoanalytically is obvious. However, it cannot be validly studied in isolation. If we accept that the prerogative of art is either to mirror or to perfect life, then it becomes necessary to show how the environment in which a character operates, shapes and nurtures it. Since a character is essentially a product of its environment, the study of that environment in the end leads to a better understanding of the character in the context of its world.

The concern of this paper is with character and intention[2] and, in investigating such concerns, literary criticism moves to the psychological plane since the answers which such enquiries must give will be based on assumptions about the workings of the author's mind. Thus, the psychoanalytic perspective remains useful primarily because it is concerned with both obvious and concealed meanings in art and investigates the various ways in which an artist transforms fantasy material, considers ways in which genres control such fantasy material and generally justifies the unconcealed interest in the conscious and the unconscious life of the artist in the history of psychoanalytic scholarship and criticism.

The task of this paper is to examine the ways in which Bessie Head's psychoanalytic activities have been manifested in her artistic creations. She has not only re-created herself in the characters who are projections of herself but she also re-creates herself in the other sense of breaking down her personality and remoulding it, thus creating more vibrant and much more 'successful' variations of herself in art. Her earlier works and many of her short stories are all autobiographical to varying degrees and reveal the novelist biographically and psychoanalytically.

The issues of nationality and the stateless status of the author hauntingly pervade these works. Her protagonists help to reinstate the theme of alienation from race and state. Although Margaret Cadmore in *Maru* ostensibly belongs to a tribe, the Masarwa, of greater and more far-reaching importance is the fact that others see the Masarwa people as sub-human. This rejection of Margaret and her people as viable individuals tallies with the rejection by society of the author and her biological mother. Makhaya and Eugene occupy key positions in the sections of the South African societies from which they hail. Yet they are both loners willing to accept the challenges of deciding their own destinies unaided by society. They survive as strangers in the midst of their respective racially contiguous societies. Like these two, Maru finds the prevailing social situation into which he is born a chief's son irksome and alienating. As with the others, in deciding his own destiny, he carves out a lone and different path for himself.

All Head's major protagonists are forced to accept an isolated status before they can realise their true destinies. As in her own personal situation, the sublimation of desires subtly appears as alienation and makes the attendant positive gains, or the creative civilisation of this form of alienation, realisable. Gilbert's alienation from his family and his eventual seclusion in the woods provide the haven of his utopian dreams which he finally brings to fruition in Golema Mmidi. Eugene does as much for the native people of Motabeng as Gilbert does for those of Golema Mmidi but he too had to first cut himself off from where he was thought to belong – that is, the exploitative Afrikaner ruling class of South Africa – before he could contribute meaningfully to humanity. Finally, in order to make a permanent and effective statement that will forever change the status of the Masarwa, Maru cuts himself off from his people and his inheritance.

All these fictional fragments are in reality a working out of an aspect of the novelist's dominant psychic condition. Her forced isolation in high school led her into the 'magical world' of books as she herself intimates.[3] However, she did not write anything for which she is known and remembered today until she broke finally with South Africa and settled in Botswana. Until her death in 1986, Head lived much of her life in this adopted home as a stranger. Yet all her achievements were made under these circumstances. And writing aside, it is here that she fought and won the war of personal survival. This picture of intense and effective creative and emotional work undertaken in extremely difficult conditions is a recurring theme in her works.

There is also an uncompromising suppression of the parenthood of the major characters in these works, especially that of the father. Thus, the unconscious reinstatement of the author's orphanhood is effectively conveyed. Maru is a chief's son whose father is never seen or even heard of; virtually nothing of Makhaya's family is known other than that he is the first child and so occupies a highly respectable position in his family. We learn about Gilbert's mother's disappointment at Gilbert's size and ungainly gait, yet nothing memorable is said about his father. Again, no mention whatsoever is made of Margaret's biological father. Expectedly, all these characters work out their fates without the slightest consideration for their parents, especially their fathers. This total black-out of the father figure is Head's psychological way of dealing with an image which she never as much as glimpsed in her own life.

II The novelist's personal history and the unwholesome social realities into which she is born form the nucleus of the psychotic condition present in her life and works. The pictures of her nightmares so poignantly conveyed in *A Question of Power* have caused the publishers of the novel to describe it as a book which takes the reader 'in and out of sanity'.[4] Significantly though, the writer has remained undaunted despite the rancour over the text. In her 'Return Notes to Joby Dean on *A Question of Power*' she asserts:

> I am not such a fool as to waste my energies on a truly unprintable book. The gain I had on my side was that psychology itself would understand that sort of book due to what has been uncovered by the psychiatrists about the unconscious.

Implicit in this is a plea for a psychoanalytical reading of the text. And in attempting this, the proper place to begin would of course be to establish the relationship between Elizabeth, the heroine of the text, and Bessie Head, its author. Elizabeth's mother, like Bessie Head's, was a white woman who had been confined to a mental home because she was to have a child by a black man who was also a paid servant in her father's house. Much of the material relating to the author's background in various studies is largely gleaned from pages 15 to 19 of *A Question of Power* and has been corroborated by vital authorial statements.[6] The major fault with the novel in this regard is the narrative point of view employed. Head has written that the character of Elizabeth is herself and that the text is a record of 'a private and philosophical journey to the sources of evil'.[7] One would then have expected such a personal story to be told in the first person which would limit the author/narrator to what she knew, experienced, inferred or could find out by talking to other characters.[8] It is quite possible, as Pascal asserts, that by using the third person point of view, an autobiographer posits an objective relationship to himself and thereby misrepresents the true character of life as seen from inside.[9] Fortunately, the author opted for the limited point of view which allowed her to tell the story in the third person, confining her nonetheless to what was 'experienced, thought and felt'[10] by Elizabeth alone. This journey on which the author takes her reader is of interest to the scholar/critic as its examination provides information on the moulding agents that formed and shaped the personality that is Bessie Head.

The mission principal unwittingly set the young Elizabeth on the long tortuous journey into painful alienation by informing her of the true circumstances of her birth. Concerning this aspect of her life she was later to write in her 'Biographical Notes':

> I harboured a terrible and blind hatred for missionaries and Christianity which they represented and once I left the mission I never set foot in a Christian Church again. (96)

But while still at the mission school, Elizabeth often 'sat in a corner reading a book' (*AQP* 16) for she had learnt to look inward and was thus introduced to the magical world of books as the only peaceful companionship she could enjoy. This hobby ultimately sowed 'the seeds of her writing career' to borrow Lee Nichols' words. And as the autobiographer puts it:

> I did a lot of reading on my own because I love that particular world. You open up a book and you learn about something that's much more exciting than your everyday grind, a world of magic beyond your own. And I feel that the beginnings of writing really start wherein you know that when you open a book there's a magical world there.[11]

Although she left the mission school equipped to be a school-teacher, the love for a writing career had equally taken root.

The sequence of events in *A Question of Power* shows how they help in the peculiar moulding of the character of Bessie Head. These events are used to inform her peculiar religious inclinations and also to explain the foundations of her life's vocation in writing. The pivot of her psychological struggle is the issue of her search for identity – a sore issue on which she speaks quite frankly and touchingly:

> The circumstances of my birth seemed to make it necessary to obliterate all traces of a family history. I have not a single known relative on earth, no long and ancient family tree to refer to, no links with heredity or a sense of having inherited a temperament, a certain emotional instability or the shape of a fingernail from a grandmother or a great grandmother. I have always been just me with no frame of reference to anything beyond myself.[12]

Makhaya may be different, being a Zulu born into a traditional African home, but Margaret Cadmore is virtually in the same position as Elizabeth. For Margaret:

> there seemed to be a big hole in the child's mind between the time that she slowly became conscious of her life in the home of the missionaries and conscious of herself as a person. A big hole was there because, unlike other children, she was never able to say: 'I am this or that. My parents are this or that'. (*Maru* 15)

Elizabeth moved to Botswana in the hope of finding a new home to which she could belong. Although it is true that, unlike South Africa riddled with general aggression, 'there was a flow of feeling [in Botswana] from people to people [and] people here were kings and queens to each other,'[13] nevertheless, the issue of total acceptance was quite another matter. We shall come back to this later, but for now let us turn again to *A Question of Power*. The novelist provides a clue to a better understanding of the text in a letter to Lee Nichols where she writes:

> The novel works at two levels – an interior narrative and the everyday life of a village in Botswana. The everyday life was deliberately juxtaposed against the interior narrative for contrast and a choice between two worlds; one of death and destruction and the other which promotes life. ... It is not basically a book about insanity.[14]

The evil in the oppressive South African social system constitutes that world of death and destruction against which she juxtaposes the near idyllic Motabeng village world which promotes life. Her protest in this novel is in the exposition of this world of death and destruction, and in her proposition on how to purge this, she presents the liberating options she is committed to. The compulsion to record evil as a way of doing away with it is ultimately an important goal of the autobiographical genre. Femi Ojo-Ade summarises this succinctly in his critique of Bessie Head where he writes:

> When the piece of writing is autobiographical, ... the reader knows that he is going to be a fellow traveller in a journey through the night into the dawn of a new day. Torture. Oppression. Depression. Optimism. Hope. Disillusionment. Despair. Final triumph. Love. Happiness. Elevation of man to his natural position of dignity.[15]

This pursuit after the successful elevation of man to his natural position of dignity is Head's primary commitment because, as she remarks, we should have 'a future which is defined for our children, a grander world'.[16] One of the author's three objectives in writing the novel *A Question of Power* is to obtain a catharsis. In writing it, she purges her life of the evil she has encountered and in so doing reclaims herself. As she puts it:

> I wrote the book in order to continue my own life and to let evil as such pursue its own course.[17]

By a truthful recording of significant events in her life, the author was able to confront the causes of her neurosis and to effect its purgation, which brings to mind Fanon's theories on alienation as concerning the African in the former European colonies of the third world. Like this African, the black South African in the apartheid system had been so 'injected with fear' as to become divorced from himself and alienated from his entire social and economic set-up. Thus, he necessarily craved to find a meaning to his existence in order to be able to justify that existence.

Bessie Head began that quest when she left South Africa for Botswana. And when she rightly delineated the contrasting worlds of South Africa and Motabeng, we recognise a readiness for the next action of rejecting the unsavoury and unacceptable.

Alienation and madness have come to be used interchangeably in modern fiction. In artistic representations where they form an essential portion of the thematic development (as in *A Question of Power*) such works have often been criticised for illogicalities and inconsistencies. However, the authors of such works resort to this manner of writing because they find it the most effective way of conveying the difficulties in comprehending the very experiences they want to record. In 'One of the Difficulties of Psycho-Analysis', Sigmund Freud remarks that:

> One has only to list the names of the great writers in the modernist pantheon in order to be reminded of how little faith they had in the power of man's reason to know and master himself and his world. The image of representative modern man that they project is man out of control.[18]

Cataloguing these major writers, he concludes that each:

> has given rise to the assumption that the heroes of our spiritual life necessarily live precariously, on the outer edge of sanity, teased out of mind by the irrationality in the world.[19]

The social circumstances of Elizabeth and her distinctive ideological biases place her among the select group of writers who may be deemed 'heroes of our spiritual life'.

There is a pattern to the 'madness' often associated with *A Question of Power* as a text. The infinite juxtaposition of the real with the internal 'insights, perceptions, fleeting images and impressions [which have] required more concentration, reflection and brooding than any other work she (the author) had ever undertaken' (*AQP* 29) constitute what many term the mad or dream portions of the text. Encapsulated in these perceptions, insights and reflections are much of the rudiments of the writer's critical and ideological perspectives. These internal insights and reflections provide the bedrock for her ethical and moral stands as they concern her socio-political commitment. From these, we glean her rationale for her 'doctrine of ordinary', for instance. Being 'essentially a product of the slums and hovels of South Africa [where there is the] unwritten law to hate any black person among them who was important' (*AQP* 26), Elizabeth is forced to recognise that 'one of the most complete statements for the future a people could ever make' was

> Be ordinary. Any assumption of greatness leads to a dog-eat-dog fight and incurs massive suffering. (*AQP* 39)

By extension this doctrine of ordinary encapsulates the author's humanistic world view which comes out in her attempt to tackle religion and other related moral issues in *A Question of Power*. As she puts it:

> The whole book works hard at the idea of breaking down the image of an
> almighty and supreme being and towards a universal sharing of the image of
> goodness, thus mankind as such is generally regarded as being sacred or holy if
> you work on my theory. ('Bessie Head on *A Question of Power*' 18)

Rukmini Vanamali's study based almost exclusively on the mythic
dimension of this text is useful on many counts. It is the first to give the
work a religious reading. And significantly, it demonstrates that at least a
basic knowledge of Hindu philosophy and Eastern religions can be
helpful if the burden of unravelling and understanding much of the 'mad
world' in that novel is to be lessened. However, if one's reading gravitates
towards the christian God as the universal God instead of Osiris or Rama
or Krishna, then the inevitable conclusion which must be reached is that
the novelist's achievement in this area is at best modest. Her attempt to
work on a religious angle largely accounts for the difficulties in the text.
Much of the religious philosophies used do not appear properly understood and are not meaningfully conveyed. Probably, the novelist's confrontation with the overwhelming societal ills of South Africa, worsened
by the apparent lack of justice, leads her to conclude that the image of an
Almighty, All-Wonderful and All-Perfect God is but illusive, and that, at
best, this figure is only barely existent in one's mind and even then only
as an ineffectual and sometimes even hateable figure who allows the
most awful things to happen to the people he professes to love. Although
such an agnostic stance may seem reasonable, it must be said that only
an improper understanding of the christian God can explain such
diffidence.

The writer has not succeeded in breaking down this image of an
Almighty God and it is difficult to accept that she has worked hard on
this. She has two different images of the God figure: one is that of real
human beings, residents in particular societies from which they have
learned humility and have emerged as humane. On the average, these
figures are cast in the images of godness. Buddah, Sello and Elizabeth
belong here and so do Eugene and Makhaya. However, these people are in
no way substitutes for the supernatural, all-knowing God whom she calls
on instinctively in times of trouble and to whom she actually confesses.[20]

The broad definition of God which she formulates and employs
Elizabeth to reveal to us is that:

> God is the totality of all great souls and their achievements; the achievements
> are not that of one single, individual soul, but of many souls who all worked to
> make up the soul of God, and this might be called God, or the Gods. (*AQP* 54)

It is, in fact, this which explains why she arrogates a God-like status to
many of her protagonists. And on the basis of this perception, she makes
a distinction between christianity and God, both of which have since
become 'courteous formalities people had learned to enjoy with mental
and emotional detachment' and the 'real battle front (of) living people,

their personalities, their treatment of each other' (*AQP* 66). Her pragmatic conclusion tersely put forward is that

> A real, living battle of jealousy, hate and greed was more easily understood and resolved under pressure than soaring, mystical flights of the soul. (*AQP* 66)

Men and women who help themselves and others to resolve these must then be given precedence over and above the mystical God. Her stand is that the distant or remote god who to all intents and purposes is insensitive, is better relegated and sensitive and humane men projected instead.

Ironically, even if this humanistic stand sounds anti-christian, it is in fact not so. The Holy Bible teaches that we cannot in all honesty claim to love God whom we cannot see when we hate our brother whom we see and that he who hates his brother is indeed a murderer (1 John 4:20; 3:15). Leigh Hunt's widely acclaimed 'Abou Ben Adhem' reinstates this biblical stand for, although Ben Adhem was not listed among those who love the Lord, he was yet listed first among those 'whom love of God had blessed' because he loved his fellow men.

The positive function to be accorded madness is that it is itself a natural way of healing our own appalling state of alienation called normality[21] and the descent into madness is a mythical journey from which one can and does return with a special knowledge and ability.[22] The successful representation of her struggles completes the writer's cathartic experience. And as she tells us, 'from the degradation and destruction of her life had arisen a still lofty serenity of soul nothing would shake' (*AQP* 202). Evidently, *A Question of Power* is Bessie Head's *Bildungsroman*. It begins with the intimation of the details of her birth, spans the South African socialisation processes, exposes the details leading to her writing career and humanistic world view and then unveils her philosophical growth into a universal personality.

III In contrast to *A Question of Power*, the other two texts under study, that is, *Maru* and *When Rain Clouds Gather*, are fictional autobiographies because they are products of a combination of the autobiography and the novel. The novel may be taken to mean that fictitious element which is 'the method by which ... thought develops into action ... (and where) the dominating feeling is of an existence where every thing is intentional'.[23] Through the protagonists in these novels, Bessie Head works out more successful variations of herself.

When Freud remarked that the 'royal road' into one's unconscious will be the examination of one's dreams, he used the term dream to denote visionary pictures and thoughts which one experiences in one's sleep. It is not possible to discuss dreams in this sense with regard to Head's works. In the first place, there are no dreams as such in this text. And then again the novelist/narrator confesses that at some point 'the dividing line between dream perceptions and reality was to become confused' (*AQP* 22). Thus, it will be unprofitable to try to delineate Elizabeth's dreams in this sense.

It will be more useful in the context of this study to discuss dreams as 'something only imaginary; a distant hope or ideal probably unattainable'.[24] Admittedly, fantasies help writers to enjoy in fiction what had been denied them in actual life and satisfies a longing for the good life. Margaret Cavendish, Duchess of Newcastle, who wrote the first female autobiography in English, *True Relation*,[25] and a utopian fantasy, the *Blazing World*, justifies self-realisation in this sense when she writes:

> Although I have neither power, time nor occasion to conquer the world as Alexander and Caesar did; yet rather than not be mistress of one, since Fortune and Fates would give me none, I have made a world of my own for which no body, I hope will blame me since it is in every one's power to do the like.[26]

Successfully animated wishful thoughts abound in Bessie Head's works and the most easily recognisable one is in the final working out of blissful matrimonial relationships for her protagonists. From her lived experience, she did not have a successful married life. As a personality, she was neither obviously strong nor dominating and, in fact, she describes herself as 'just this loosely knit shuffling ambiguous mass' which was her personality. Yet she confesses of *When Rain Clouds Gather* that the 'male character obligingly serves the author'[27] and of Maru that 'a whole portion of it was myself, my African background'.[28] Both Makhaya and Margaret could be seen in fact as idealised portraitures of what the novelist would have liked for herself. The author's celibacy was not wilfully chosen. In an interview with Paddy Kitchen, she confesses thus:

> If I were so fortunate to have a husband, be in love, I should forget all about the world and spend a great deal of time kissing. Knowing my nature, the gods condemned me to a long life of celibacy in order that the world might progress. It is not much to my liking.[29]

It is only to be expected then, that there is a noticeable departure in the author's handling of Margaret's relationship with men. Margaret gets enough attention from very respectable individuals. Significantly, Maru repudiates his kingdom to seek out a new world with her. Again, the questions of belonging and acceptance do not bother Margaret because in her heart she had grown beyond any definition, she was a little bit of everything in the whole universe (*Maru*, 16). In contrast, Elizabeth had to go through four painful years of rejection in Botswana before she could nullify the power of evil (which included 'obsessive love' for her adopted homeland) through endurance and the power of the spirit, and render it purposeless and irrelevant and, in consequence, procure for herself a better alternative to formal acceptance as a Botswana citizen. Gratifyingly, we learn from a synopsis of Gillian Stead Eilersen's *Bessie Head 'Thunder Behind my Ears'* (1995) that she was granted Botswana citizenship after fifteen years. That would then be precisely five years after *A Question of Power* was first published in 1974.

Makhaya is handsome, physically attractive and decidedly assertive. Unlike Head he has a very strong personality. Yet apart from the external parallels between him and the author, he too has a wiry tenacity for self preservation and survival just like Elizabeth herself. It is easy to attribute the final and smooth working out of both Margaret Cadmore and Makhaya to the author's wishful fantasies for herself. With them she gains those grounds which have eluded her in real life.

IV In addition to these obviously autobiographical works a study of the short stories 'The Special One' and 'The Village Saint' shows them to be further artistic representations of Head's life and hopes. Gaenametse, the Special One, suffers the kind of anguish which Elizabeth's husband subjects Elizabeth to in South Africa. Both men thoughtlessly flout their marital vows and luxuriate in licentious adultery. For Elizabeth, this proves the last straw in South Africa; for Gaenametse, it reduces her to alcoholism and madness. Both pictures are in reality two faces of the same coin. Although Elizabeth does not succumb to alcohol and madness in South Africa, these prove simply to be waiting in the wings. They take their toll in Botswana when she confronts a projection of her dreaded husband now emerged as Dan. Dan's numberless women and Elizabeth's traumatic experience at their hands parallel the emotional battering forced on her by her South African husband. This time predictably, she succumbs to both alcohol and madness just like Gaenametse.

However, it will be a limited viewpoint to seek to trace all manifested psychoses in Head's works solely to unsuccessful male/female relationships. As Tennenhouse points out, in order to do a sophisticated character study in psychoanalysis:

> It is important ... to understand the nature of the external world which the character encounters and the kind of demands that the external world makes as the character struggles to deal with the range of his or her needs.[30]

It behoves the scholar-critic in all cases and especially in psycho-analysis therefore, to see the work of art as a product of an individual psyche within the context of a particular historical and cultural setting. For a character and writer who is as humane as Bessie Head, the South African society is to say the least maddening. Elizabeth, Makhaya and Eugene live in South Africa initially with the hope of achieving something for themselves. However, they all soon get disillusioned over time and come to see all their hopes and expectations as mere illusion, the ultimate realisation being that no matter what goodness was displayed, in deed or thought or word, the result remained discouraging and continued to be so until one came to terms with the fact that just too much was required from one, so much that one could not safely give. Such societal effects are as debilitating for men as for women, for husbands as for wives.

The human reaction to this set-up had been neurosis in its many and varied facets. For some it manifested as quiet withdrawal and alienation; in some others, such alienation culminated in madness. Yet for most, neurosis had the most devastating thanatos effect resulting in suicide and murder. This is the nature of the external world from which Elizabeth springs. It is a world effectively depicted in the style in which Head writes *A Question of Power*. Elizabeth's extensive and reckless use of stimulants, such as cigars, alcohol and sleeping tablets, is an index of the kind of self-destruction which the society induces. The demand which the external South African world makes on its citizens are such as spell fatal results. Two *Drum* stories of May 1967 and May 1975 help to illustrate the enormity of the situation. On 6 September 1966, forty-eight-year-old Demetrio Tsafendas stabbed to death Dr. Hendrik Verwoerd, then South African prime minister. Tsafendas was a trusted member of Verwoerd's race and was thought harmless enough to be allowed close contact with the prime minister. Ironically, though, Tsafendas

> was a crazy mixed-up product of South African society, where race tension, colour prejudice and sheer unhappiness lie near the surface like nerve ends ready to be exposed in an instant. ... a lone operator who committed the murder with the fevered casualness of a split personality, a product of the instability of an unhappy society. [31]

It did not matter that he was a member of the Boer race – a people purported to be privileged.

Seventeen-year-old Frank Hearne's story is even more pathetic. Although born to coloured parents, he turned out to be more white than coloured and finding that hanging between white and coloured was far more frustrating than being just coloured, he committed suicide:

> Frank Hearne used to live in South Africa. Near Cape Town. He tried to be coloured. He wasn't. He tried to be white. He wasn't. Frustrated, he took his own life. [32]

The madness of the entire system is very adequately conveyed by the cryptic remarks, 'he tried to be ... he wasn't, he tried to be ... he wasn't.' Hearne's story is of particular interest because, like Hearne, Elizabeth could not and did not fit comfortably into any particular race category. She saw herself as an African but was never accepted as such. This racial rejection accounts for half the emotional stress she was saddled with and had to bear.

Stories such as these help one to understand Laing's contention that societies can on their own manifest symptoms of psychosis[33] making it only possible for an individual to 'experience himself in despairing aloneness and isolation'.[34] Elizabeth and Gaenametse retract from their societies, relocate themselves away from the others and there rediscover themselves. Thus, proving, as Laing argues, that withdrawal from an inhospitable and unhomelike world is a sane and reasonable method of self preservation.[35]

Dan, his thunderbolt releasing Medussa as well as Mma Mompati are in reality displaced representations of aspects of the oppressive system in which the author lived. Dan epitomises phallic oppression and Mma Mompati, female betrayal, the two oppressive evils the novelist had to battle with in real life.

The point which Head makes successfully in these stories is that plain wilting women, with seemingly weak personalities, can have strong and adoring partners. Gaenametse becomes the Special One to her spouse and Mompati breaks off his overwhelming devotional attachment to his mother for Mary's sake. Like Dan, Mma Mompati in the short story 'The Village Saint', 'understood the mechanics of power'. For one, that is Dan, we learn that

> From his gestures, he clearly thought he had a wilting puppet [that is Elizabeth] in his hands. Once sure of that, he never cared a damn what he thought and did.(*AQP* 13)

And for the other, Mma Mompati, not even her 'polished etiquette and the professional smile of the highborn' could belie the fact that she does not 'really give a damn about people or anything'.[36] Mary Pule 'a thin wilting, willowing, dreamy girl with a tremulous voice whom her son had married',[37] turned out to be the tool the author uses to unmask Mma Mompati's facade of fastidious holiness. She 'secretly despised the weak wilting plaintive little wretch her son had married and needed to dominate and shove the wretch around'.[38] And when she finally does strike out at Mary, it is with what the novelist significantly describes as a 'thunderbolt' (*The Collector of Treasures* 18). Interestingly, and as was the case between Dan and Elizabeth, Mma Mompati's thunderbolt cracks Mary's facade of helplessness, revealing in its place a 'tenacious will' which Mma Mompati could neither suppress nor even match.

The difference between art and reality in these cases is that art not only mirrors life but actually perfects it. And we conclude this essay by suggesting that in the elevation of the simple and seemingly weak characters of Gaenametse and Mary Pule, the author symbolically reinstates the meek and lowly of which she is part.

NOTES

1. W. W. Meissner, 'Some Notes on the Psychology of the Literary Character: A Psycho-analytic Perspective', *Seminars in Psychiatry* 5 (1973): 261–74.
2. E.D. Hirsh, Jr, *Validity in Interpretation* (New Haven and London: Yale University Press, 1967) 1–23.
3. See Lee Nichols, *Conversations with African Writers* (Washington DC: Voice of America, 1981) 55. Hereafter cited as *Conversations*.
4. See the back cover of the African writers series edition of the text published in 1974 by Heinemann.
5. Bessie Head, 'Return Notes for Joby Dean on *A Question of Power*', *The Times Educational Supplement*, 11 September 1970.
6. (a) *Conversations* 55, (b) 'Bessie Head on *A Question of Power*', Letter to Lee Nichols (VOA retired) *ALA Bulletin* 12 (3) (Summer 1986): 17.
7. Bessie Head, 'Social and Political Pressures that Shape Literature in Southern Africa' *World Literature Written in English* 19 (1979): 24.
8. M.H. Abrams, *A Glossary of Literary Terms* Fourth Edition (New York: Holt, Rinehart and Winston, 1971) 144.
9. Roy Pascal, *Design and Truth in Autobiography* (London: Routledge and Kegan Paul, 1960) 165.
10. Abrams 144.
11. *Conversations* 50.
12. Bessie Head, 'Biographical Notes: A Search for Historical Continuity and Roots' in E.N. Emenyonu (ed.) *Literature and Society: Selected Essays on African Literature* (Calabar: University of Calabar, 1986) 96.
13. *AQP* 21 and 72.
14. 'Bessie Head on *A Question of Power*', *ALA Bulletin* 12 (3) (Summer 1986): 17.
15. Femi Ojo Ade, 'Bessie Head's Alienated Heroine: Victim or Villain', *Ba Shiru* VIII (1978): 14.
16. 'Bessie Head on '*A Question of Power*', 17.
17. Ibid., 18.
18. Sigmund Freud, 'One of the Difficulties of Psycho Analysis', in *On Creativity and the Unconscious* (New York: Harper, 1958) 13.
19. 'One of the Difficulties', 13.
20. *AQP* 39, 131, 149.
21. R.D. Laing, *The Politics of Experience* (New York; Random House, 1967) 116.
22. Laing 25.
23. E.M. Forster, *Aspects of the Novel* (1929 rpt. Harmondsworth: Penguin, 1982) 58.
24. *Chamber's 20th Century Dictionary*.
25. *A True Relation of my Birth, Breeding and Life*, appended to *The Life of William Caven-dish, Duke of Newcastle*, ed. C.H Firth, Second edition (London: n.d). I owe my know-ledge of this work to Mary G. Mason, 'The Other Voice; Autobiography of Women Writers' in James Olney (ed). *Autobiography: Essays Theoretical and Critical* (Princeton: Princeton University Press, 1980) 207–35.
26. *A True Relation* 178.
27. 'Biographical Notes' 98.
28. *Conversations* 52.
29. 'Interview by Post: Paddy Kitchen has been corresponding with Bessie Head', *The Times Educational Supplement*, 11 September 1970: 13.
30. Leonard Tennenhouse, 'Introduction' in *The Practice of Psycho-analytic Criticism* (Detroit: Wayne State University Press, 1976) 13.
31. *Drum*, May 1967: 25 (Not paginated originally, page supplied by the author).
32. *Drum*, May 1975: 14.
33. Laing, *Politics of Experience* 8.
34. R.D. Laing, *The Divided Self* (New York: Random House, 1969) 15.
35. *Politics of Experience* 79.
36. Bessie Head, *The Collector of Treasures* (London: Heinemann, 1977, rpt. 1986) 14.
37. Head, *The Collector of Treasures* 17.
38. Head, *The Collector of Treasures* 17.

```
┌─────────────────────────────────────────────────────┐
│  Afterword                                           │
│  Editing African Literature Today                    │
│  1968 to 2001                                        │
│                                                      │
└─────────────────────────────────────────────────────┘
```

Eldred Durosimi Jones

The first number of *African Literature Today* which came out in 1968 was the result of a confluence of enthusiasms: mine for the new literature of Africa, that of Heinemann Educational Books, which had the largest list of African writers and that of James Currey, Keith Sambrook and Alan Hill, who looked after that pioneering list. The journal had been preceded by a much humbler cyclostyled *Bulletin of African Literature* which was a direct result of an African Literature Conference held in Freetown. The purpose of *African Literature Today* was to provide a forum for the examination of African literature to open the literature to both academic and general readers particularly within Africa itself. In the words of the first editorial: 'It is the critic's business to read discerningly and demonstrate the qualities of a work and thus (a) to make it accessible to a larger readership than the absence of criticism might have opened to it, and (b) by an accumulation of such examinations to help establish literary standards.' That editorial also cited the hope of John Povey, a pioneer critic of African literature: 'that African critics can ... play a special role in the interpretation of their own literature'. Over the last thirty-three years, many African scholars have had their earliest critical work published in it and have gone on to higher things while the journal has gone some way to providing a body of critical opinion against which the literature can be studied. Fortunately non-African contributors have also brought new perspectives into the examination of the works of African writers, thus enriching the critical literature.

The first four numbers came out as issues of a journal with articles on a range of topics. It was then decided that from number five each annual number should be organised as a book around a theme by which attitudes to general issues by the creators of the literature, who so often were conscious of their role as teachers, were aired. Issues on Women, Language, Orature, and Childhood, revealed both traditional attitudes to various aspects of life as well as the writers' own particular reactions to such attitudes quite purposefully intending to influence, or even change them. This transformed the whole enterprise in that the issues of the journal continued to sell and on occasions reprint. For instance, number ten, which came out in 1979, is still selling today as a book, unlike a journal which rapidly dates.

These thirty-three years have been for me an adventure which has brought me into contact with a wide variety of scholars, associates, advisers, many of whom have become personal friends. I edited the first eleven numbers by myself always with the anonymous help of my wife who had painfully typed the stencils of the preceding *Bulletin*. I was joined for numbers twelve to nineteen by my colleague at Fourah Bay College, Professor Eustace Palmer, and since number twelve, now acknowledged on the cover, by my wife, Marjorie. I have also received valuable advice from my Associate Editors – Professor Emmanuel Ngara, Dr Nnadozie Inyama, Professor Simon Gikandi, Dr Ato Quayson, Professor Francis Imbuga and my Reviews Editor, James Gibbs. The warm associations with contributors were probably due to my preference for personal letters over reply cards in reacting to submissions. Even rejection letters often contained suggestions for improvement and resubmission either to me or to other journals. This, in turn, generated a volume of friendly correspondence which sometimes included details of family life, marriages, births and successes from correspondents whom I have never met or have run into only long years after our meeting on paper.

Editing a journal in Africa over periods of instability with breakdowns in postal services, with colleagues in colleges and universities suffering declining facilities, produced some almost paralysing situations. My publishers too, in seeking favourable conditions sent manuscripts over vast distances in various stages of production. We had to get the manuscripts to them for copy editing and queries, and they had to send them for typesetting to one corner of the world, for printing to another, back to us for proofreading and indexing, then back to the publisher for final production. Many are the slips that can occur in this process and more than once a whole edited manuscript has just vanished. Oddly enough one such disappearance took place within a distance of no more than a couple of miles as the crow flies. The effort of re-eliciting manuscripts from authors dispersed over vast areas was hair-raising. The only copy of one edited manuscript was lodged in the Post Office on a Saturday only for a military coup to intervene on the Sunday thus freezing the copy for several weeks until, through the diplomatic skills of my wife, it was retrieved from the sealed Post Office.

Editors in technologically advanced countries enjoy the luxury of stipulating strict standards for the formatting of articles for publication, failure to meet which results in almost automatic rejection. We too hopefully required such standards, but would have been doing a great disservice to reject potentially good articles whose authors had difficulty in meeting such standards, access to typewriters and even the right size of paper being sometimes problematic. We have even received manuscripts in handwriting! On the other hand, we have received not only perfectly computer typed manuscripts but some even accompanied by diskettes! Our aim has been to encourage criticism so that when a potentially good article has weaknesses either in the construction, or in the treatment of bibliographical references and notes, wholesale re-writing has been necessary and almost always with the grateful acknowledgement of the original authors. In this process, I have myself learnt a great deal about African literature, about criticism and about writing.

When James Currey left Heinemann in 1984 to set up his own publishing company in Thornhill Square, London, *African Literature Today* moved with him and Kassahun Checole's Africa World Press took over the co-publishing in North America. The warm personal association between editor and publisher blossomed even more. Friendly business lunches rustled up by Clare lubricated the meetings. Keith Sambrook later left Heinemann and added his experience to James Currey Publishers. These meetings moved in 1996 to Botley Road, Oxford, where with Lynn Taylor and Douglas Johnson, the family atmosphere continued. The relationship between editor and publisher has enabled us to triumph over the problems of long-distance editing and the severance of this relationship will be for us the saddest feature of my giving up the editorship. But life must go on and we are happy to hand over to one of *African Literature Today's* earliest contributors, Professor Ernest Emenyonu, who, coincidentally, will be working with his wife. We wish them and the journal as happy a period in the editorial chair as we have had.

Note by James Currey

Eldred and Marjorie Jones managed to keep *African Literature Today* running for a third of a century. So many of the journals which were founded in Africa in the brave new sixties have not survived. *African Literature Today* has always had a majority of contributions from within Africa itself. Their meticulous editing ensured an international reputation in Africa, in Europe, in North America and throughout the rest of the world.

Eldred Jones makes light of the personal dangers and difficulties which have resulted from life in Sierra Leone in recent years. At one stage their house was being fired through by the Nigerian peacekeepers on one side and the rebels on the other. At another time Eldred and Marjorie Jones joined a delegation to Guinea to try and negotiate peace. On one occasion they had to return overland from Guinea. I said that it sounded like Graham Greene's 'Journey without Maps'. Eldred Jones replied that for much of the way it was a 'Journey without Roads'.

Violet Barungi, *Cassandra*
Kampala: Femorite Publications, 1999, 256 pp., £6.95/$11.95, ISBN 9970901044.

Jane Kaberuka, *Silent Patience*
Kampala, 1999, 228 pp., £5.95/$9.95, ISBN 99709010720.

Goretti Kyomuhendo, *Secrets No More*
Kampala, 1999, 168 pp., £5.95/$9.95, ISBN 9970901052.

Regina Amollo, *A Season of Mirth*
Kampala, 1999, 117 pp., £5.95/$9.85, ISBN 9970901060.

All titles distributed by African Books Collective, 27 Park End Street, Oxford, OX1 1HU, UK

The four novels reviewed here were all published by Femrite Publications, the publishing arm of the Association of Ugandan Women Writers. It is independent, non-profit-making and vigorous. It has gender-related aims and appears to be very successful in encouraging women writers. Mary Karooro Okurut, its founder and chairperson, is a lecturer at Makerere University, a prolific writer herself and is galvanising many others, as well as these four. Violet Barungi is Deputy Editor of *New Era*, a Femrite magazine. Jane Kaberuka is a senior civil servant and this is her third novel. Goretti Kyomuhendo is Femrite's coordinator and has enjoyed participation in the University of Iowa's International Writing Program. Her first novel is reviewed in ALT 21. All three are Makerere graduates and have been writing for some time. The fourth is a pediatric nurse, currently working in Eastern Uganda, with a significant knowledge of the area. This is her first novel. All write about communities with which they are familiar and are concerned with the relations between men and women, parents and children, and family as well as other issues in a changing society. Three of the four novels are set in affluent urban surroundings but are aware of the disturbed life of the modern world. Barungi's story is mainly set in the city. Kyomuhando begins in war-torn Rwanda and her conclusion involves a personal domestic peace only. Kaberuka begins in the country, and has not ignored traditions, but the story comes to the city, goes overseas and moves towards a sense of nationhood and a future not devoid of hope. Amollo looks at the widening world from a village.

There has been much discussion in East Africa about the responsibility of writers to the community. How far should they be 'committed'? Can they discuss the beauty of the Western hills rather than the scourge of AIDS? If a writer belongs to an organisation such as Femrite it must be tempting to feel so strongly about gender issues that the writing becomes one-sided, leaning towards propaganda. These writers all have a story to tell and are rarely diverted into preaching a cause. All have a lively approach, although there are occasional lapses in credibility: for example, I find the sleepwalking seduction in *Cassandra* hard to believe. Linguistic weaknesses are certainly irritating. One may accept the Ugandan 'I finished to do...' if the character is speaking English not very well, and, indeed, rather stilted dialogue is a fact among relatively fluent second-language speakers. But in narrative, or when the characters must be assumed to be speaking their mother tongue, the language should be standard. Just as a little more research into detail of medicine, for instance, would increase our belief in the many injuries and illnesses that occur.

The eponymous heroine of *Cassandra* is a modern woman ambitious for a career. She reveals the problems facing a girl in a male-dominated world, and her emotional vulnerability as a beautiful woman is emphasised. She falls in love with the handsome Raymond, who is divorced with a son he loves deeply, but she is made pregnant in the sleepwalking scene already referred to, by Raymond's brother. Her husband, a completely selfish man getting by on good looks and charm, knows he is sterile, but is able to convince himself that Benjie is his child. The interlinked families in this well-to-do urban setting are clearly portrayed, as is the way in which the turbulent 1980s affected individual lives. But the portrait of the young men is not entirely convincing and one is aware of the puppet-master's hand as Raymond's son dies, and as he himself has a terrible car crash and later dies. Brother Bevis is shot, leading to the eventual happy ending of the love story, but by that time one feels there have been rather too many bedside scenes. One is glad that Cassandra's career has flourished, that she has a happy marriage and a family in the end. There is a wide canvas of characters, mostly young professionals. They entertain in a sophisti-cated fashion and suffer from the instability of relationships that has hit urban society in many parts of the world. However, it seems a rather narrow, inward-looking group, the dialogue is stiff and the book would certainly benefit from editing.

Silent Patience has greater control of plot and a wider canvas but would also be improved by judicious editing. The story is told by Stella, but the device of daughter Agnes's letters home enables a widening of viewpoint

as the story follows the odyssey of Stella who leaves school for a successful, arranged marriage, and the responsibilities of an extended family, in a
semi-rural setting. Agnes has a successful career, becoming the first
female Minister of Health. However, both mother and daughter suffer emotionally. There is friction in Stella's marriage and the male tendency to
unfaithfulness often causes tension. All this is very complex and a reconciliation results only when the pair are open with one another. However,
their new beginning is aborted by a car crash which kills both husband and
a younger daughter, leaving her pregnant with a son. Agnes suffers the
problems of secondary school and University, falling in love with a married
man by whom she has a child but who abandons her when she is disfig-
ured through heroically saving the baby from a chip-pan fire. She eventually marries the young (wealthy) doctor who really loves her and puts
her first while Stella too is courted and at last enjoys marital happiness.

The story is set against a period of political upheaval, and the Tutsi
background of the protagonist, tribal frictions and exclusionism, and the
changing attitudes in a fairly affluent part of society, both rural and urban,
are clearly presented. The obstacles to a happy ending are somewhat con-
veniently removed, but horrific car crashes, armed robbers and untimely
deaths are part of the Ugandan pattern, and the resolution suggests hope.
The characters sometimes seem a bit pompous with their philosophising
but the title is justified when Stella finally is able to marry the young man
she liked at school but who came from a different tribe. It is appropriate
that the final conversation should be looking to a brighter future which
they hope to create.

Secrets No More has a protagonist who is the only survivor of a massacre in
Rwanda. Marina is the only child to escape after she has seen her mother
raped and killed, her father killed and her siblings murdered. The story
has only just begun when she finds her way somehow to a refugee camp in
a state of trauma. Here Father Marcel takes an interest and she is placed in
an orphanage where she slowly recovers. Her charm and competence win
her privileges but, at a stage when all seems to be going well, she allows
herself to be seduced by a young man, and begins her secondary school
career by becoming pregnant. The resulting child, Rosario, is taken to the
orphanage where the priest arranges her care, and Marina finds a new home
with a pleasant, childless couple. Through them she meets George
Walusimbi. George is an interesting character who has been led into crime
almost by accident. The corruption of urban society is again evident and
George and Marina have secrets from one another. Marina goes to the
mission to see Rosario, and marries George in the hope that in due time she
can give her child a home. George's ill-gotten affluence produces unhappi-
ness for Marina. Among uncongenial house-guests, Dee, who is there to
plan revenge on George for his sister's death, attracts her. But, before the
budding attraction can provide an escape (and a home for Rosario), George

has a terrible accident after Mrs Magezi tells him Marina's story, ironically in the hope that it will help their relationship! Marina stays until he discharges himself from hospital, by which time she feels neither loyalty to him nor real love for Dee. Father Marcel has made her his heir and she can now make a home for herself and her daughter. Dee, it is clear, was not her solution – they had mistaken sexual attraction for love. The death of Father Marcel makes her independent although completely alone. Small wonder that she concludes: 'Yes, everything had been a mistake from the beginning ... her parents shouldn't have been killed, Matayo shouldn't have raped her ... George should have been told the truth, Dee and her was a mistake.' She leaves the house in tears. George commits suicide. Dee goes to France. There is, however, a happy ending in an epilogue: the widowed Magezi, whose wife died of a stroke, cares for her and they marry. One more secret remains – because he was infertile Magezi's child was the result of IVF. (Incidentally, the question of fertility occurs in several novels.) Here there will be no child. There are interesting characterisations although the links are not completely dovetailed. Father Marcel's coming to Africa is linked with his indulgence of Matayo. Sister Bernadette's past history adds depth to the presentation of the Mission characters but surely she ought to have been more clued up on pregnancy? When the story of George is to be developed, we move so far from what has happened that it seems a different narrative, and its integration into the main thread is clumsy. The plot is packed with violent incidents and emotions. The ignorance of the young people in the early part of the story contributes to their disasters and one is very aware of the violent and corrupt city in which they live. There are plenty of interesting talking points, but we tend to look at them all from the outside.

Of all these novels, the one that remains vividly in the memory is *A Season of Mirth*. Instead of a wide time-span, numerous inter-linked family stories, and a sophisticated lifestyle, the author concentrates on a single season in one village and the neighbouring market town. Amollo focuses on one simple family and their relations and neighbours. The details of daily life ring true and the author has a real appreciation of the setting coupled with the ability to describe it. For instance, as the bridegroom's family collect the young bride, we read: 'The sun was moving towards the west. It had left the middle of the sky, making the shadows long. The bitterness had gone out of it.' Obvious, you may say, but it reflects the mood, and we share a life which measures time by sun and moon.

Okanya and his wife, Abeso, have two daughters and a smallholding. Each has a part to play in the home where Okanya is very definitely the head, but where his wife is able, within limits, to manipulate him. His daughters cooperate to allow Anaro, the older daughter, to go to a dance when he would not initially allow it. It is here that she meets the young policeman son of a neighbour, who then follows the traditional pattern of courtship to marriage when she moves to Kampala.

There is a stability and a rhythm about this life which is sadly missing in the context of the other novels, and the transition from a small community seems less pretentious and more sustainable. When Anaro brings presents home they are soap, sugar, salt and tea. She has heard of 'Mafuta' (the fat which the wealthy enjoy) but Ewiu has a policeman's salary. Okanya is something of a despot: he sits on a chair at a table while the women sit on the floor; he drinks too much and can be both aggressive and infuriating. But there is a genuine family here. They have deep family feeling and it is a joy that Abeso is able to produce a son. Interestingly, to pick up the fertility theme, Abeso conceives after her nurse friend prescribes medicine to help menstruation, and after her 'wise woman' friend gives her leaves to 'sweeten' her husband. The story is told simply, and from the viewpoint of the women.

It is the meticulous detail and the truth of the character portrayal that makes this novel so enjoyable. It equates in a way with the impact made upon this reader many years ago by *Things Fall Apart*. It is instructive of a way of life which is changing but told through a thoroughly interesting story about a group of people with whom one feels sympathy, even with the infuriating oracle. The book's strength lies in the truth of the characterisation and the interlinking of the different activities. Readers are allowed to make up their own minds, assess the strengths and weaknesses of this plain rural life, and begin to think how to keep the best of it in a time of change.

The title *A Season of Mirth* is a true description. One revels in the essential natural rhythms that can incorporate the friction of gender, or sibling rivalry, of health problems, the need to reconcile indigenous and imported medicine, while maintaining a stable society. If a teacher wants to raise gender issues Amollo's is probably the most effective of the novels to discuss.

This is a truly heartening crop of novels to come out of Uganda. There is added pleasure in the original and lively cover designs, and in the recognition given to the artists. Unfortunately, however, the standard of proof reading and general editing needs improvement. There are misspellings, words omitted and sometimes worse. In the last novel, we are seeing Anaro and Ewiu off with drumming and song when, in mid-sentence (page 83), we find we are with Abeso and Rose at the clinic! And on a different level – how far should an editor allow Ugandan English when it deviates from standard and jars on the reader? Should we accept 'A knicker' or 'a trouser' as an acceptable regional form? Each writer has her own style but all could benefit from careful editing, even of such basic matters as syntax, spelling and punctuation. I understand that some educationalists in Uganda are sufficiently bothered that they are setting up a consultancy. Good luck to them.

Margaret Macpherson
Makerere University and Windermere

Mpalive-Hangson Msiska. *Wole Soyinka: Writers and their Works*
Plymouth: Northcote House Publishers Limited, 1998, 98 pp.
ISBN 0-7463-0811-6, pbk, £8.99; 780746308110, hbk

In *Wole Soyinka*, Msiska penetrates the conundrum and unveils the crusader and mythopoet who have mystified critics and excited eulogists. The book implicates Soyinka's responses to personal experiences in Africa and Europe in his themes and politics and in the formulation of an aesthetic system that embodies the uncomfortable tensions of cultural and political hybridisation. It explains Soyinka's engagement with the violence of power and language, his satiric denigration of authority and angst over the uncritical reception of African and European canons. Msiska indicates that Soyinka's redemption of brutalised Africa and his championing of cultural and racial equality are engaged without necessarily rejecting the existence of problems and contradictions, without even belittling the importance of his attacks on pre- and post-colonial Africa.

The book investigates Soyinka's mythogenesis, and his juxtaposing of traditional African and post colonial constructs. It locates the Nigerian writer's dramatic ideas in the exploration of binary oppositions, arguing that Soyinka's individuality as playwright lies in his careful selection and fusion of African and European forms into a new language that is at once tragic and comic, humorous and serious, and 'which, in some important ways, resembles the symptomatic readings proposed by Pierre Macherey'. (79. See Macherey, *Manichean Aesthetics*, 1983). These features provide Soyinka's writings with their critical edge, their caustic language and poetry, their piquant and disturbing characterisation.

Msiska elevates Soyinka's characterisation to a contested site for the interrogation of cultural imperialism and selective hybridity. This examination reveals the soft underbelly of some apparently heroic figures, African and European. It also universalises evil, not as 'an attempt to rationalise the failings of pre-colonial Africa, but as a subtle way of avoiding falling into the trap of logic' of Abdul Jan Mohammed's 'Manichean dichotomy'. This portrays colonial Africa as 'embodying an essential barbarism that is in absolute opposition to an inherently civilised Europe' (55–6).

The book's five chapters suggest an integrated, thematic reading, dispensing with the individual textual analysis and strict generic delineation adopted in other studies. (Moore, *Wole Soyinka*, 1978; Ogunba, *Movement of Transition*, 1975.) Chapters are presented as broad thematic pictures, drawing related themes together from different chronological periods, dramatic and literary genres, autobiographical and critical writings. This approach does not substitute broad generalisations for deep study since Msiska weaves the themes and sub-texts of different works into a common frame through Soyinka's stylistic handling of theatrical metaphor and idiom. The resulting reading explains Soyinka's handling of mythology; it defends him against the charges of obsession with myths and of deliberate mystification.

The introductory chapter foregrounds the development of Soyinka's literary and dramatic styles in the tensions brought about by the meeting of different cultural and educational traditions. The second chapter, 'Satirical Revelations', depicts the satirist whose gift paints a tragic but humorously disturbing picture of Africa, one which challenges received ideas about Africa and Europe. 'Tragic Comedies and Comic Tragedies' explores Soyinka's satirical and grotesque characterisation, and the humour in otherwise tragic circumstances in such works as *The Interpreters* (1965), *Death and the King's Horseman* (1975) and *Madmen and Specialists* (1971). Msiska insists that 'it is (in) the transcendence of the distinction between the tragedy and comedy that Soyinka excels in the texts just mentioned, always attempting to explore new possibilities of dissolving the boundary between the genres and reconstituting them as fluid zones of generic identity exchange' (52). 'Redemptive Tragedies' interrogates Soyinka's fusion of Aristotelian paradigms and African theatrical modes of the tragic to explore the human condition and the nature of political and social evils in post-colonial Africa. It investigates Soyinka's belief in the futility of isolated struggle and the redemptive suffering necessary if we are to dare to hope. The conclusion reveals the humour and satire in Soyinka's biographical writings while throwing light on some of his lesser-known works.

The book's few unfortunate errors include misidentifying the corruption of the policeman in *The Road* with apartheid South Africa's racist Pass Laws: extortion by corrupt Nigerian policemen often involves invalid or forged documents. In addition, Msiska misdates Nigeria's first military coup (1966), misinterprets the position of the Oba in Yorubaland and misses the role of the tragic protagonist in *Death and the King's Horseman*. Perhaps the major charge that can be levelled against the book is that the language, while generally effortless, is on occasions convoluted and excessively academic. Despite these flaws, the study offers a deep, intelligent reading of Soyinka's works. It is extensively-researched, the broad themes are sufficiently interrogated and each idea is significant.

Victor I. Ukaegbu
University College, Northampton, UK

Osonye Tess Onwueme. *The Missing Face: Musical Drama for the Voices of Colour*

New York & Lagos: Africana Legacy Press, 1997, 64pp. £4.25, $7.95 pbk
ISBN 1-57579-053-X

Distributed by African Books Collective, 27 Park End Street, Oxford, OX1 1HU, UK

The Missing Face examines the dilemma of diaspora blacks whose feelings of cultural alienation are matched by a longing for identification with an almost mythical motherland whose love they question and whom they ultimately hold responsible for their plight. Set in Idu (Igboland, Nigeria), a symbolic African Kingdom, and in Milwaukee in the late 1990s, the play explores the mystical, and almost heroic, journey of Ida Bee, an African-American woman, and Amacchi, her son, in search of Momah, her US-educated husband and the father of Amaechi. For Ida Bee, the bringing together of father and son is a sacred duty; for in the very act of securing Amaechi's identity in Africa lies his salvation from the cultural fragmentation and spiritual vacuity of African-Americans. Armed with the half-face of an Ikenga carving (an Igbo symbol of spiritual authority) and her dead father's instructions to find the other half and unite the sections, Ida Bee's personal quest becomes the collective odyssey of those in the Black diaspora to re-establish their African roots. In the process, through Ida Bee's and other black women's heroic struggles to sustain family and cultural identities among African-Americans, Onwueme foregrounds her interrogation of African patriarchy.

This musical drama is divided into seven movements symbolic of the stages of the annual Iwu festival of passage into manhood. Its tempo is fast, ensuring smooth transitions, and it is deployed to link different chronological periods. Afuzue/Griot embodies the roles of historian and storyteller, and his physical presence bridges time gaps, limiting the necessity for explanatory dialogue or extensive plot development. Ida's flashback to Milwaukee and to her meeting with and marriage to Momah draw the past, present and future into a confrontation that is resolved only in the enduring strength of Africa's restored links with those in the diaspora. It is only in the ritual act of collective purification and rebirth that Momah's generation can identify with the strong, recast and bronze Ikenga proudly borne by Amaechi and the future generation.

Though Onwueme's censure of the uncritical imitation of Western civilisation lacks the biting satire found in Wole Soyinka's presentation of Lakunle in *The Lion and the Jewel*, the complex symbolism of the final meeting of Africa's separated essences is superbly handled. Somewhat weakened by a reductionist approach, Onwueme's dramaturgy nevertheless yields an enduring theatre enhanced by symbolic representations: Ida's journey and encounters with Africa, her purgatorial banishment and re-integration foreshadow Africa's spiritual re-birth. The foreshadowing invests the festivities and rituals, the props and the characterisation with symbolic, archetypal significance. The play's convincing portrayals of Igboland and Milwaukee; the former in the gripping moment of celebrating its sense of community, and the latter recalled through the violence of American society, give the play a unique ambience of arresting spirituality and cultural depth. It becomes a paradigm of black people's collective search for self-restoration and identity.

The *Missing Face* draws on such African theatrical idioms as masking, storytelling and ritual. The dialogue combines wit with discursive narratives, as the play rushes to a somewhat predictable but theatrically rewarding resolution. The reliance on types unfortunately limits conflict and character development to a semiotic signing resulting in two unfortunate developments. First, apart from Ida Bee and Odozi, characters lack the depth to match their almost heroic actions. Second, the incest between Momah and Ida Bee is not interrogated as the resolution subordinates this serious cultural abnormality in Igbo society to collective identity. Despite this unfortunate resolution and the unconvincing presentation of Momah's motives, the play is exciting for its proposals on Africa and African-American relations, and for its deft integration of African and Western theatrical forms.

Victor I. Ukaegbu
University College, Northampton, UK

Festus Iyayi, *Awaiting Court Martial*
Lagos, Benin, Jos, Oxford: Malthouse Press Limited, 1996. 255pp., £6.25, $10.00, pbk, ISBN 9-78260-179-9.

Distributed by African Books Collective, 27 Park End Street, Oxford, OX1 1HU, UK

Awaiting Court Martial is a collection of fifteen stories set in the bewildering climates of individual and collective apathy and violence, social degradation, official corruption and repeated betrayals by political leaders in Nigeria. Though the stories are set predominantly in the Bendel and Delta areas, the careful selection of incidents and characterisation enlarge the scope and topicality of the stories to embrace the whole of Nigeria. This makes the tales and their individual locations symbolic reference points for all peoples and societies marginalised and brutalised by a combination of self-inflicted social and political forces.

Iyayi's collection is one of the increasing number of books chronicling the misrule of a richly endowed economy by corrupt politicians and a military oligarchy that has abdicated its traditional responsibilities. Iyayi blames the military and its violent, dictatorial, corrupt generals for

Nigeria's problems. His style is refreshing and individual. At different times, he is either storyteller and victim as in 'Awaiting Court Martial' and 'Saira', or participating audience as in 'Three Times Unlucky' and 'Extracts from the Testimony'. In these stories, Iyayi offers society a closer look at its suffering victims and the emptiness of their oppressors. Despite the stories' common relationships and their differing explorations of individual and collective culpability for the country's problems, Iyayi's characters are not pawns pushed around by circumstances. They are sufficiently confronted with choices so that their individual decisions are predicated on self-will. Iyayi indicts both leadership and citizenry, bully and victim; he blames all and exonerates none. His open-ended resolutions challenge readers to examine their motives and actions before reaching hasty judgements, and he refuses to pass judgement himself. The tales leave a haunting presence of evil and unnecessary pain, a harrowing pessimism that is matched by the harshness of the titles, and only tempered by the fragile hope and optimism of the very short closing story, 'Sunflowers'.

The title story, 'Awaiting Court Martial', 'Jegede's Madness', 'When they came for Akika Lamidi', 'Noruwa's Day of Release I and II', 'Flora's Reply' and 'Sunflowers' deserve special mention for their themes, for Iyayi's deft handling of the storytelling medium, and for his masterful treatment of plot and suspense. The common theme is anticipated and almost predictable, yet the different plots take readers on twisting, unexpected journeys that defy comfortable conclusions. Herein lies the particular significance of the stories and the effectiveness of Iyayi's style, for despite, or because of, the traumas associated with the incidents and characters, the conclusions are astonishing. 'Awaiting Court Martial', 'Saira' and 'When they came for Akika Lamidi' explore the torture and helplessness of the victims of corrupt leadership and their institutionalised agents. 'Jegede's Madness' and 'Noruwa's Day of Release I & II' expose the culpability of individual actions in the workings of fate. Both sets of stories explore individual motives but 'Flora's Reply' questions the craving for remedial action despite consciously deciding against good and right. Iyayi attempts to rekindle optimism in 'Sunflowers', but the general thrust of the stories is to expose the vulnerability of virtue, and to show the resourcefulness of evil. The only real hope for Iyayi's society is a collective will to resist evil.

Iyayi's language is straightforward and clear. Though enriched by cultural metaphors and symbols, it is sometimes over-elaborated and overly descriptive. Social fragmentation is investigated from different perspectives, with the narrative generally lending itself to a critical exposition of human excesses. The conclusions are powerful and shocking, sometimes bewildering. The stories challenge society and individuals to consider political and social change as the only alternative to the present situation.

Victor I. Ukaegbu
University College, Northampton, UK

Chibo Onyeji, *Polite Questions and Other Poems*
Enugu, Nigeria: Fourth Dimension Publishers, 1998. 70pp., £2.95, $5.50, pbk.
ISBN 9-78156-445-8

Distributed by African Books Collective, 27 Park End Street, Oxford, OX1 1HU, UK

This collection explores contemporary racism against Africans in Europe. Chibo Onyeji defies racist arguments while celebrating Africa against a background of racist misrepresentations. The titles of the collection's five parts, 'Polite Questions', 'The Letters', 'Memoranda', 'Moments', and 'Afrobeat', indicate the thematic unity and structural development of the poems from well-mannered acceptance of European platitudes, through rejection to the robust espousal of Africa's identity.

'Polite Questions' believes that the interest displayed by Europeans in Europe-based Africans shows Europe's fortress mentality, while 'Masquerades' exposes the racism of white supremacist activities. 'Living Among You', 'Colour of Difference', and 'Marathon Man' implicate European interventionism in Africa and the European Union respectively for fostering racial intolerance and for the very intercultural exchanges Europe laments and undermines with acts of racism. In 'Neighbours' and 'Faces of Africa', the poet firmly rejects Europe's demonisation of Africa and the repackaging of the continent for tourism and economic exploitation. 'Black Panther' defends Africa and defies the racist undertones in her relations with Europe. This defiance carries through into the letters in Part II, a set of direct, evocative addresses to individuals and institutions. 'Letter to A Brother' advises Africans on race relations while 'Letter to the US of A' presents America as the model of racial tolerance and cultural inclusiveness.

In 'Memoranda', and especially in 'The Black Scientist' and 'Cold Distance', the poet questions Europe's claims to racial and intellectual superiority. In the process, he reveals the artfully concealed racism beneath the veneer of respectability. Part IV, 'Moments', recalls the nobility and greatness of traditional Africa. 'It Wasn't the Hangman's Axe' laments Africa's hopeless faith in Europe's interventions, and appropriates the execution of Saro-Wiwa by the Abacha military junta in Nigeria as a political metaphor for Europe's purely economic interests in Africa. In 'Odabo (goodbye) Fela', the only poem in the closing section, 'Afrobeat', the poet laments the neglect of Africa's identity and traditions in a fitting tribute to musician Fela (Anikulapo) Kuti, a man whose life and philosophy mirrored his pride in his African identity.

Onyeji's direct exposure to racism fuels his opposition to the racial categorisation of Africans in Europe. His use of repetition and snappy syntactic arrangements give most of the poems a sing-song quality, while the African and European symbols and metaphors create a harsh dialectical exchange that mirrors racial relationships between the two continents.

Victor I. Ukaegbu
University College, Northampton, UK

Richard Boon and Jane Plastow (eds), *Theatre Matters: Performance and Culture on the World Stage*
Cambridge: Cambridge University Press, 1998, 203 pp., pbk
ISBN 0-521-63443-1

Martin Banham's contribution to world theatre deserves honour and celebration and *Theatre Matters* provides both. The delightful pun in the title, on the ono hand, asserts that theatre matters, and on the other, suggests matters of or in the theatre. The title also indicates the diversity of theatre practices discussed. Wole Soyinka's letter to Banham in which he describes his experience with the 'garrison kids' in a production of *The Beatification of Area Boy* in Jamaica, provides a perfect foreword to a collection of essays which explore how theatre is used in different cultural and socio-political contexts to make a contribution to society. All the essays – nine of them with an introduction by Plastow – argue that theatre really is important and has always been so since dramatists and theatremakers are usually out to make a statement about the state of affairs in the society, about human lives and human relationships and the socio-political and cultural pressures and contexts under which these lives and relationships are lived and experienced.

Five of the essays deal with literary dramatists and themes, two are about theatre whose usefulness resides in the practicality of presentation, while the other two look at 'theatre of conscientization'. Apart from minor mistakes such as 'yielded' instead of 'wielded' on page 7 and the misspelling of Tess Onwueme's name on page 9, Plastow's introduction successfully argues that 'theatre that "matters" must be theatre in interaction with society'. She also points out the often narrow reliance on literary theatre by Western scholarship, which one should point out has in the past led to misconceptions, and the exclusion of certain, especially non-script based, theatre practices from academic study and analysis. While one agrees with Plastow that the effectiveness of theatre lies not in the texts, but in live performances which bring audiences, performers, playwrights and theatre makers together in a shared experience, one is disappointed that the collection is biased towards studies of literary dramatists and script-based practices.

Osofisan argues effectively that the theatre-for-development approaches are not enough in themselves as 'they are not only riddled with self-contradictions, but are fundamentally insufficient to provoke the desired change to a macro-society without some additional intervention' (15). The playwright, he believes, has a role to perform even though he may be exposed to personal danger in a post-colonial military state like Nigeria. He therefore suggests that the artist can become a 'cultural guerrilla' who achieves effectiveness through 'surreptitious insurrection' (17). But seductive as he tries to make his reasons for choosing an educated audience, and in spite of going for 'topical and emotive' subjects, there is always the risk that a theatre informed by this choice may become elitist and thus pass over the heads of the 'ignorant' majority, who by implication cannot on their own change society. Steadman cleverly continues the pun of the book's title. On the one hand, he talks about racial themes in South African theatre, while on the other, he argues that race is central to South African theatre and he is worried about the deep nervousness about race-thinking or speaking which can result in an undervaluing of 'the extent to which race still matters in post-apartheid South Africa'. More significantly, he highlights the danger of an 'Africanist' viewpoint which conflates concepts of African and black as if they were synonymous, for, as he rightly says, the idea of a homogenous African identity or culture is a myth resulting from a rhetoric of an ancestral African purity.

Lyn Innes' essay, apart from its dubious Eurocentric assertion that North American Indians on isolated reservations had 'absolutely no exposure to a theatrical tradition', is a perceptive analysis of Derek Walcott's *Dream on Monkey Mountain* and Tomson Highway's *Dry Lips Oughta Move to Kapuskasing*. She argues that both are dream plays which, though not directly political, work subliminally to 'manipulate the psychology of the individual spectator, instead of attempting to change political opinion or foster specific action' (78–9). She suggests that, despite the fact that the aims and social results which the two dramatists are after are far more subtle, this in no way makes their work any less effective when compared to the more politically strident or problem-oriented dramas. Carol-Anne Upton looks at the French-speaking Caribbean theatre through the political and aesthetic philosophies of Aimé Césaire, Frantz Fanon and Daniel Boukman. She considers the way Boukman interrogates Césaire and Fanon in his theatre, especially in *Orphée negre*, which, on the one hand, is a repudiation of the ideology of negritude, and on the other, a homage to the artistic vision of Césaire. Woodyard's essay looks at the theatre of Ricardo Halac in which the playwright 'confronts and interprets the many arbitrary governmental decisions and processes' (178). Halac's theatre, Woodyard points out, was designed to achieve a political end through giving his audience the message that 'it was necessary to denounce and resist an unjust society'.

Plastow and Tsehaye examine the use made of theatre by the EPLF to further the Eritrean cause as well as raising awareness of other issues. The authors, using two plays by Aferweki Abraha and Alemseged Tesfai, argue that propaganda theatre has been used by many liberation and political movements to win hearts and minds. However, they feel that the two plays discussed manage to go beyond the crude agit-prop and prescriptive style of most propaganda theatre by respecting and trusting the intellectual capability of their audiences. Srampickal and Boon see the work of the Social Action Groups as being to make people aware of the social, economic and political issues which affect their lives, with interventionist theatre playing an important role in this process of mass conscientisation. The SAG theatre projects achieve this through post-performance discussions and follow-up action, and it is this which gives them an advantage over street theatre groups. The main body of the essay analyses the methodologies of SAG theatre, highlighting its strength which is its accessibility to and concentration on the rural poor and lower castes; and also its weaknesses which include the superficiality of the analysis of the issues presented. Another weakness which the authors identify is a prevalence of 'themes of grim oppression, and clichéd plots' which, they rightly argue, can 'only serve to emasculate revolutionary potential and strengthen fatalistic attitudes' (148). It is debatable just how successful the celebratory theatre they recommend can be, but I agree with their argument that merely using the myths and folk forms of the communities is not enough to empower the villagers. They must become part of the play-making process, not just passive consumers whose viewpoints are not represented.

Interrogating the practices of Tara Arts and Tamasha, Verma adopts the term 'binglishing the stage' both to signify the inevitable 'negotiation between English and Indian [Asian] languages and sensibilities ... in contemporary England', and as a site for the 'invention of a distinctive Asian theatre identity' in England. For Verma, the 'translations' and 'quotations' of European texts by these and other Asian theatre companies set up a kind of 'dialogue with England' in which notions of self, 'Other' and 'Outsider' are confronted and articulated, either through Tara's 'creative correspondences with the "other"' or through Tamasha's presentations of 'slices of the other'. Heritage's essay is inspired by Augusto Boal's search for a functional theatre. However, he goes beyond the 'romance' with this exotic but energising philosophy of theatre that both interrogates the practice, and uses it as a starting point for journeys into other theatrical domains and practices. In the process, he raises most of the questions which scholars and practitioners seem to want to ask about Boal's work. He concludes that the latter's 'writing and teaching' are merely promises for the future, which like most promises are rarely kept. Heritage finds in the work of Nos do morro, a theatre company based in Vigidal, a hillside *favela* in Rio de Janeiro, a company that differs from Boal in that it seeks to 'create a theatre that is in no sense useless, but makes no direct allusion to its usefulness as commentary or agitation' (163). The value of this theatre is that its plays act 'as a register of individual and collective social histories' which 'gain a wider resonance in the collective story-telling and remembering that forms part of this process' (163). These two essays, unlike the first five but a bit like the last two, are more concerned with the practical usefulness of the theatre process than with themes.

Together the practitioners and practices, whether literary or improvisatory, studied in *Theatre Matters*, aspire to make their respective societies better, to help individuals to see more clearly, and understand better the nature of the social processes and structures which affect their lives. The book certainly contributes to the growing literature of 'theatre that matters' across the world, especially because of its cross-cultural approach and for the fact that the theorising of the manner of this usefulness has been attempted in some of the essays.

Osita Okagbue
University of Plymouth, UK

Edde M. Iji, *Black Experience in Theatre Vol. 1: The Drama of Human Condition*
Makurdi (Nigeria): Editions Ehi, 1996. 106 pp., pbk
ISBN 978-2177-12-1

The idea of a unique black experience expressed in and through theatre as well as the idea of 'a drama of the human condition' promised in the title of Edde Iji's *Black Experience* are both quite appealing and exciting. But, alas, that is all one gets – a promise, mostly made tedious, but ultimately denied by poor organisation, oftentimes atrocious writing, a general lack of proper concept definition and realisation and inadequate editorial midwifery or rescue. His many shortcomings notwithstanding, one must praise the vision of the author for undertaking such a bold cross-Atlantic project as this.

The book is in five chapters. The first looks at 'Visions of Black Experience' in plays by J. P. Clark-Bekederemo, Amiri Baraka and Ola Rotimi. Up to a point, the chapter does a good analysis of the chosen scripts. Iji unfortunately does not tell us why these three dramatists or plays were chosen. What for instance unites the experiences of the characters in the Nigerian plays with those in the American one; or what is uniquely black about them? No link is provided apart from the generalised title of 'visions of black experience'. Chapter Two looks at three black female dramatists – Lorraine Hansberry, Zulu Sofola and Tess Onwueme – two Nigerians and one African-American. Again, no explanation is given for why these and not, say, Efua Sutherland or Ama Ata Aidoo were chosen in place of the Nigerians. The chapter heading under which the dramatists are discussed is 'Gender Empowerment' – surprising since Hansberry's *What Use Are Flowers* is not really about gender empowerment, although Sofola's *The Sweet Trap* and Onwueme's *Go Tell It To Women* are definitely about gender/feminist issues. *A Play of Giants*, Wole Soyinka's vitriolic satire on African dictators, is the subject of Chapter Three. Even though Iji provides a competent reading of this play, the chapter also suffers from poor writing, over-generalisation and unnecessary extrapolations which are supported by neither the texts nor the author's arguments. The comparison between the African dictators and Hitler, Stalin, and Mussolini is true enough, but one has difficulty understanding what the author means by the '[kaleidoscopic] revolution of Boris Yeltsin'(66) and what resemblance this bears to the coup which ousts Kamini, one of the dictators in the play.

Chapter Four on Fatunde definitely echoes both Paulo Freire's *Pedagogy of the Oppressed* and Augusto Boal's *Theatre of the Oppressed*, even though these sources are never acknowledged. Mention is made of Sartre, Du Bois and Marx without any uniform or relevant perspective provided for integrating their philosophies into the argument of the chapter or the book. Iji uses *No More Oil Boom* and *Blood and Sweat* to show Fatunde's broad African concerns and to criticise his prescriptive Marxist approach to a subject which may better be viewed through other ideological prisms. This charge is wholly justified since the Marxist approach to socio-economic configurations is often narrow and thus sometimes inadequate to cope with African situations which are essentially different from the European ones which Marx theorised for.

The final chapter presents Osofisan's *Yungba-Yungba and the Dance Contest* as a useful 'parable of change'. It starts with a refutation of 'a [glib] theory, based on racial stereotype ... that Africa and Africans are incapable of tragic conception or appreciation of tragedy ...'(87) as demonstrated by the tendency of African audiences to laugh at tragic moments in a play. Unfortunately, this is not taken further, as no attempt is made to explain what African tragedy is, just a list of great tragic plays, novels and characters which includes Kongi of Soyinka's *Kongi's Harvest*, of all people. This however does not obscure the perceptive analysis of a play in which Osofisan asserts that democratic principles always existed in African societies. This chapter suffers most from Iji's tendency to extrapolate – often using provincial play texts to make grand pronouncements or conduct polemics about political and social situations all over Africa and even the world.

The author's attempt to use a handful of Nigerian dramatists and two African-American ones to represent the 'black experience' seems arbitrary and narrow. Furthermore, there is no central thesis around which the book is argued with the result that the chapters are separate essays, united only by a common authorship and the fact that they all happen to be about black dramatists. This apart, one really struggled to read *Black Experience in Theatre*, which at best only managed in parts to conduct passable analyses of some plays. Part of the problem is that the author tries but lacks the necessary language discipline to handle the complex discourse he has embarked upon. Perhaps it would have been a better book if he had restricted himself to simply looking at how his chosen playwrights explore the black experience locally or universally. This, I believe, would have prevented the hectoring and unnecessary polemic in which he sometimes engages. This could have been a very useful book on black and African theatre, especially a comparative look at the theme of a diasporic black experience in theatre, but sadly, a weak conceptual framework, compounded by the chronic and sometimes unbelievable errors of grammar and syntax which litter the whole book, made reading neither easy nor particularly enjoyable. There are also some incorrect entries such as 'Arthur' for Athol Fugard.

Osita Okagbue
University of Plymouth, UK

Index

143

NEW SERIES *African Theatre*

edited by Martin Banham
James Gibbs & Femi Osofisan

Reviews Editor Jane Plastow
Associate Editors Eckhard Breitinger, John Conteh-Morgan,
Hansel Ndumbe Eyoh, Frances Harding, Masitha Hoeane,
David Kerr, Amandina Lihamba, Olu Obafemi & Ian Steadman

African Theatre, an annual publication, provides a focus for research, critical discussion, information and creativity in the vigorous field of African theatre
and performance. *African Theatre* also carries reports of workshops, a Noticeboard of events and news, book and theatre review sections and the
text of a previously unpublished play from an African writer.

'An exciting development...' – *Research in African Literatures*

RECENTLY PUBLISHED
African Theatre in Development
'*...a "must have" for anybody interested in issues relating to theatre and development in Africa.'*
– Sola Adeyemi in H-AfrLitCine@h-net.msu.edu
'...a valuable source on the latest developments in theatre in Africa.' – H.net book review
African Theatre: Playwrights & Politics

IN PRESS
African Theatre: Women (Guest Editor: Jane Plastow)

CONTRIBUTIONS ARE INVITED FOR
African Theatre: Southern Africa (Guest Editor: David Kerr)

Articles should not exceed 5,000 words and should be submitted double-spaced on hard copy and disk. Illustrations may also be submitted if accompanied by full captions and with reproduction rights clearly indicated.

Material should be sent for consideration to:
The Editors, *African Theatre*
8 Victoria Square, Bristol BS8 4ET
Fax: 44 (0) 117 974 4137

James Currey Publishers 73 Botley Rd, Oxford, OX2 0BS, UK